GIANT BOOK OF PENCIL PUZZLES

By
PETER GORDON, MIKE SHENK,
MAYME ALLEN, JANINE KELSCH,
MARK DANNA, JAMES RICHARD SUKACH,
& The DIAGRAM GROUP

Sterling Publishing Company, Inc.
New York

10 9 8 7 6 5 4 3 2

Published In 1999 by Sterling Publishing Company, Inc.
387 Park Avenue South, New York, N.Y. 10016

Material in this collection was adapted from
Solitaire Battleships
© Peter Gordon and Mike Shenk
Little Giant Encyclopedia of mazes
© The Diagram Group
101 Word Games
© Mayme Allen and Janine Kelsch
Word Search Puzzles for Kids
© Mark Danna
and
Challenging Whodunit Puzzles
© James Richard Sukach

Distributed in Canada by Sterling Publishing
c/o Canadian Manda Group
One Atlantic Avenue, Suite 105
Toronto, Ontario, Canada M6K 3E7
Distributed in Great Britain and Europe by Cassell PLC
Wellington House, 125 Strand
London WC2R 0BB, United Kingdom
Distibuted in Australia by Capricorn Link (Australia) Pty Ltd.
P.O. Box 6651, Baulkham Hills, Business Centre,
NSW 2153, Australia

Sterling ISBN 0-8069-2091-2

CONTENTS

TRICKY TRIOS

GENERAL INSTRUCTIONS

For the games that follow, list as many words as you can, using the designated letters in the sequence specified. You can use only one form of each word—for example, *telegraph* shouldn't also be listed as *telegraphing*. Words with different meanings, however, such as *desert* and *desertion*, can be used, even if they have the same root. No proper nouns allowed in these games.

Solutions—Pages 207-209

1 "EGR"

The letters "egr" appear in this sequence in at least 25 words—list as many as you can.

2 "OXY"

The letters "oxy" appear in this sequence in at least 21 words—list as many as you can.

3 "ADI"

The letters "adi" appear in this sequence in at least 90 words—list as many as you can.

4 "ERT"

The letters "ert" appear in this sequence in at least 115 words—list as many as you can.

_____ _____ _____
_____ _____ _____
_____ _____ _____
_____ _____ _____
_____ _____ _____
_____ _____ _____
_____ _____ _____
_____ _____ _____
_____ _____ _____
_____ _____ _____
_____ _____ _____
_____ _____ _____
_____ _____ _____
_____ _____ _____
_____ _____ _____
_____ _____ _____
_____ _____ _____
_____ _____ _____
_____ _____ _____
_____ _____ _____
_____ _____ _____
_____ _____ _____
_____ _____ _____
_____ _____ _____
_____ _____ _____

_____   _____   _____
_____   _____   _____
_____   _____   _____
_____   _____   _____
_____   _____   _____
_____   _____   _____
_____   _____   _____
_____   _____   _____
_____   _____   _____
_____   _____   _____
_____   _____   _____
_____   _____   _____
_____   _____   _____

5 "AZI"

The letters "azi" appear in this sequence in at least 19 words—list as many as you can.

_____   _____   _____
_____   _____   _____
_____   _____   _____
_____   _____   _____
_____   _____   _____
_____   _____   _____

6 "OQU"

The letters "oqu" appear in this sequence in at least 16 words—list as many as you can.

_____   _____   _____
_____   _____   _____
_____   _____   _____
_____   _____   _____
_____   _____   _____
_____   _____   _____

7 "ICO"

The letters "ico" appear in this sequence in at least 95 words—list as many as you can.

_____   _____   _____
_____   _____   _____
_____   _____   _____
_____   _____   _____
_____   _____   _____
_____   _____   _____
_____   _____   _____
_____   _____   _____
_____   _____   _____
_____   _____   _____
_____   _____   _____
_____   _____   _____
_____   _____   _____
_____   _____   _____

8 "LPH"

The letters "lph" appear in this sequence in at least 11 words—list as many as you can.

alpha
Ralph
Alphabet

9 "EME"

The letters "eme" appear in this sequence in at least 63 words—list as many as you can.

LETTER PERFECT

GENERAL INSTRUCTIONS

In the puzzles that follow, the definitions give clues to words that begin and end with a designated letter. The last letter of the preceding word is also the first letter of the next word. Always work in the direction of the numbers. With these puzzles, it's okay to use proper nouns.

Solutions—Pages 209-210

1

In this puzzle, the definitions give clues to words that begin and end with "T."

1. Easily understood; obvious
2. Substandard apartment building
3. _____ is fair play
4. Halloween custom
5. Fruit-filled pastry
6. Firm belief in person or thing
7. Unspoken; silent
8. One of three
9. Disposition; frame of mind
10. One who goes to the other side
11. In geometry, a nonintersecting line
12. Surgical procedure
13. Small corner tower
14. Temporary; passing with time
15. Writing paper fastened at one end
16. Absent without permission
17. William Hurt film, "The Accidental _____"
18. Multitalented individual, "triple _____"
19. Tense; not slack
20. Canvas shelter
21. Fish at the end of the rainbow

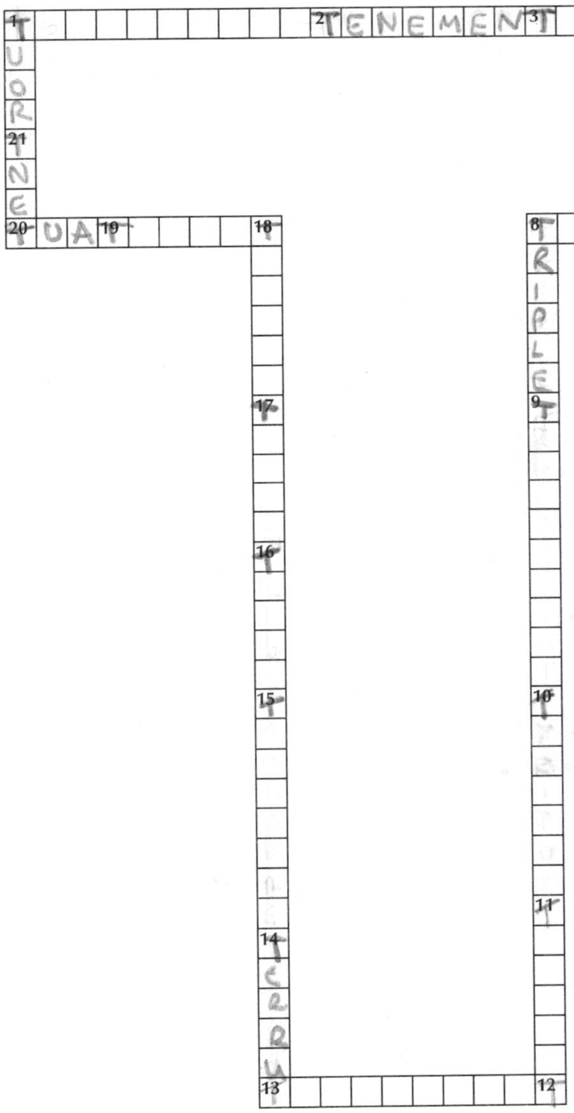

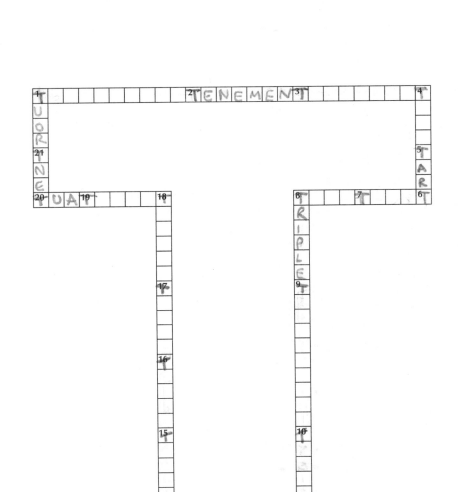

2

In this puzzle, the definitions give clues to words that begin and end with "E."

1. Baked clay containers; dishes
2. Large, imposing building
3. Small group of musicians
4. Keep apart; remove
5. Cut or etch letters on object
6. Shaky natural disaster
7. Vivid, forceful speech or writing style
8. Steal
9. Count one by one; list
10. Something that proves an allegation
11. Walkway along shoreline
12. Drive out evil spirits
13. Treat as equal
14. Roof edge
15. Slip by; pass
16. Get away from; flee
17. Free from blame
18. Tasteful and dignified manner
19. One with discriminating taste in food or wine
20. Give hope or confidence
21. French sandal or shoe
22. Bubbles in beverages
23. Teach; train
24. Insert opinions in factual article
25. Explain in greater detail

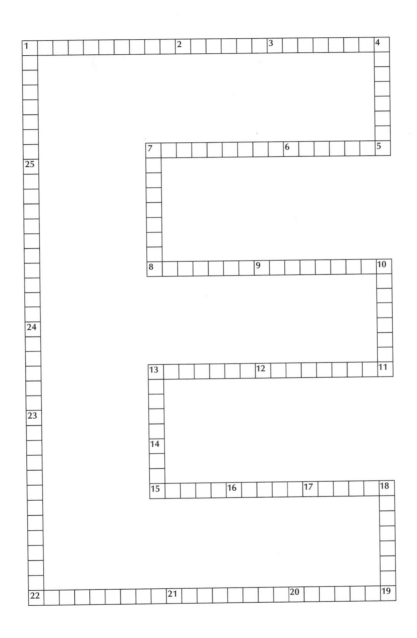

3

In this puzzle, the definitions give clues to words that begin and end with "L."

1. The Beatles' hometown
2. Garbage under layer of soil
3. Kind of evergreen shrub
4. Room deodorizer
5. Slander
6. In football, pass parallel to goal line
7. Part of the pea family
8. Political term for reciprocal voting
9. To classify as; identify
10. Opposite of conservative
11. Quiet; interval
12. Exact; precise
13. Miss Langtry's nickname
14. Faithful; true
15. Mel Gibson movie hit "_____ Weapon"
16. Lounge about
17. Listless; languid
18. Extension of jacket collar
19. Expressing feelings through song
20. Confined to a particular place
21. Uses correct reasoning

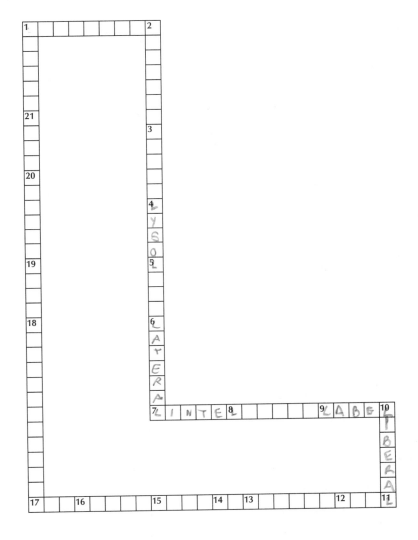

4

In this puzzle, the definitions give clues to words that begin and end with "N."

1. Female version of pajamas
2. Head (slang)
3. Has nine angles, nine sides
4. Women's stocking material
5. Male member of nobility
6. Wayne or fig
7. Colorless gas found in earth's atmosphere
8. Chemical element; component of all living things
9. Covers lap during meal
10. Famous blue-eyed thespian
11. Idea
12. Small ear of corn
13. Gary Cooper western "High _____"
14. One _____ indivisible
15. 18 + 1 =
16. 37th U.S. president
17. French general and emperor
18. Strikeout king Ryan
19. Day-old baby
20. Sister Kate is one
21. Country singer Willie _____
22. Uncharged atom part
23. Five-cent movie theater
24. Proton or neutron in atom's nucleus

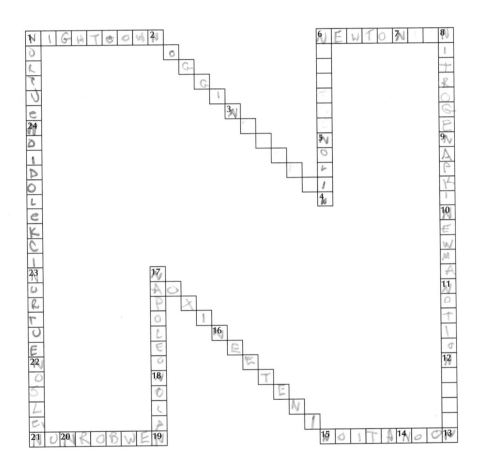

Crossword grid with the following filled entries:

- 1 across: NIGHTGOWN
- 6 across: NEWTON
- Down from 2: NOGGIN
- 3 down: N
- Left column (1 down): NURTUENDIDOLEKCIURTUENOSLEV
- 8 down: NITROGEN
- 5 down: NOON
- 4: N
- 9: NAPKIN
- 10: NEWMAN
- 11: NOTION
- 12: N
- 17 down: NAPOLEON / VAN...
- 16: NINETEEN
- 18: N
- 21/20 across: NONROBWEN (NEWBORN)
- 15/14/13 across: NOITANOO (... NATION)

5

In this puzzle, the definitions give clues to words that begin and end with "H."

1. Hip and upper thigh
2. Seasoning; plant of mustard family with pungent root
3. Situated far above ground
4. Game involving moving from one compartment to another
5. Liquor; alcoholic beverage (slang)
6. Chopped mixture of cooked meat
7. Refuse fed to farm animals; swill
8. Canopied seat for riding on elephant or camel
9. Plant of lily family distinguished by bell-shaped flowers
10. Exclamation of praise to God
11. Stone or brick floor of fireplace
12. Very short distance
13. Turkish confection of seeds and nuts
14. Woody Allen character played by Mia Farrow
15. Make quiet or silent
16. Tahoe hotelier
17. Word with same spelling but different meaning and origin
18. From this moment on
19. Premonition; feeling about upcoming event
20. Cheer; shout of joy
21. "Leave It to Beaver" star _____ Beaumont
22. Part of racetrack between last turn and finish line
23. Physical and mental well-being
24. Fasten with hook or knot
25. Drug made of Indian hemp
26. Pen or coop for animals

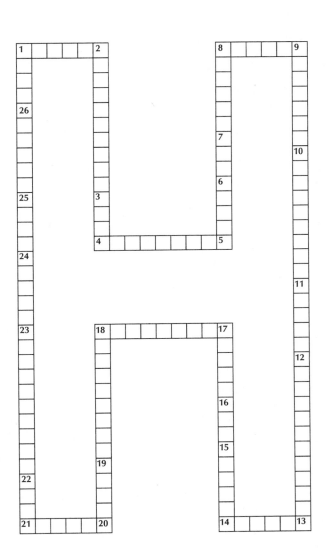

6

In this puzzle, the definitions give clues to words that begin and end with "R."

1. Person skilled at telling stories or anecdotes
2. Appointed to hold funds of others
3. Unconfirmed story; hearsay
4. Male domestic fowl
5. Extreme harshness or severity
6. Cattle thief
7. Natural stream of water
8. Water-filled device for radiating heat
9. Santa Claus' transportation team
10. Bring to maturity by educating, nourishing
11. Loud, deep, rumbling sound
12. Warden who patrols government forests
13. Savior
14. Pistol with cylinder containing several cartridges
15. French painter
16. Tool of measurement
17. Continuing, bitter hate; ill will
18. Restaurant in style of German tavern
19. Wood or metal hinged vertically at ship's stern
20. Clinging rose
21. CBS news anchorman
22. Slender two-edged sword
23. Occur again after an interval
24. Reclaim or get back
25. Give or pay as due
26. Used to indicate direction and distance of object
27. Characterized by conformity, order

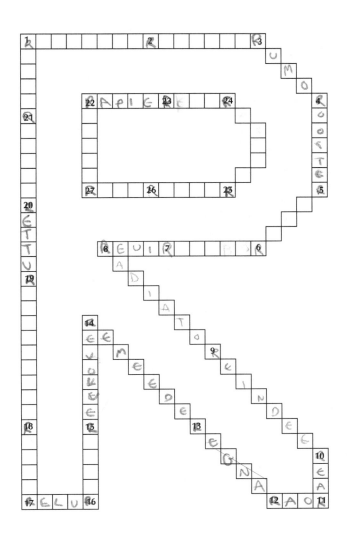

7

In this puzzle, the definitions give clues to words that begin and end with "D."

1. No longer living
2. Small dog with long body and short legs
3. Second king of Israel
4. Neglected; broken down
5. Hardest known mineral
6. Gadget; bauble
7. Wood nymph in Greek mythology
8. Stretch out; expand
9. Completely without
10. Intense fear, apprehension
11. Slight; treat without due respect
12. Sum of money divided among stockholders
13. Cartoon character _____ Bumstead
14. Automobile panel with instruments, gauges
15. The Magic Kingdom
16. Bomb that fails to explode
17. Without life
18. Misshapen
19. Country star Parton's theme park
20. Father
21. Move from higher to lower place
22. Document that states property transfer
23. Disagreement; clash
24. Mean, skulking coward
25. Member of Celtic religious order
26. Minor deity; partly divine

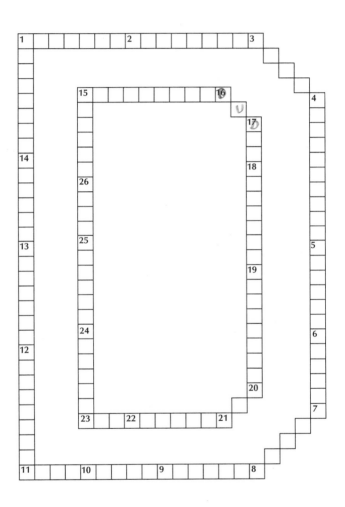

8

In this puzzle, the definitions give clues to words that begin and end with "S."

1. Disrespectful to things held sacred
2. Moved by natural feeling or impulse
3. Small telescope
4. Greek tragic dramatist
5. Phonograph needle
6. Quell; put down by force
7. Excessive; more than needed
8. Absence of
9. Working steadily; diligent
10. Strain; pressure
11. Advantageous coexistence of two dissimilar organisms
12. Italian violin craftsman
13. Contest involving common fund
14. Fond of study; attentive
15. Air carrier in skull opening to nasal cavities
16. Shameful; shocking
17. Brief, general review; summary
18. Characterized by false, malicious statements
19. Native of Switzerland
20. Having no backbone
21. Clandestine; secret

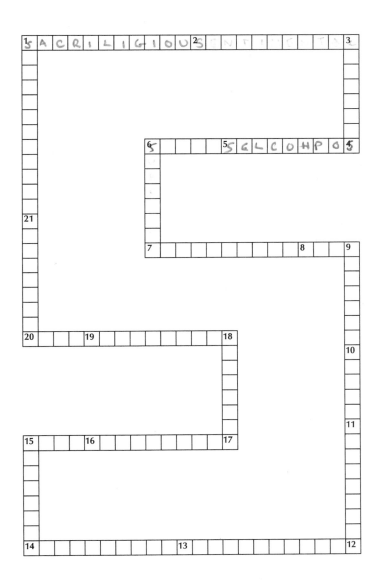

SOLITAIRE BATTLESHIPS: SEAMAN

GENERAL INSTRUCTIONS

Battleships puzzles are a solitaire version of the classic paper-and-pencil game of the same name. The object of each puzzle is to find the locations of the 10 ships in the fleet hidden in a section of ocean represented by the 10-by-10 grid. The fleet consists of one battleship (four grid squares in length), two cruisers (each three squares long), three destroyers (each two squares long), and four submarines (one square each).

The ships may be oriented either horizontally or vertically in the grid, but no two ships will occupy adjacent grid squares, *even diagonally.* The digits along the side of and below the grid indicate the number of grid squares in the corresponding rows and columns that are occupied by vessels.

The Fleet:

Battleship	▰▰▰▰
Cruisers	▰▰▰ ▰▰▰
Destroyers	▰▰ ▰▰ ▰▰
Submarines	● ● ● ●

Solutions—Pages 211-212

In nearly all Battleships puzzles, the contents of a few of the squares have been revealed to start you off. These "shots" come in four types:

Water This square contains no ship.

Submarine This square consists of a submarine, and thus must be surrounded by water.

End of a ship This square can be oriented in any of four directions. It indicates the end of either a destroyer, cruiser, or battleship. The square adjacent to the flat side must be occupied by a ship segment. All other surrounding squares are filled with water.

Middle of a ship This is either the middle segment of a cruiser, or one of the two middle segments of the battleship. Either it has the squares to the left and right occupied by ship segments and the ones above and below it empty or the squares above and below are occupied by ship segments and the ones to the left and right are empty. In both cases, the diagonally adjacent squares are filled with water. In fact, any time a square is occupied, all of the diagonally adjacent squares must have water in them, because ships can't touch diagonally.

The most basic strategy to Battleships solving has three parts:
1. Fill in what you know in squares adjacent to given ship segments.
2. Fill in water in rows and columns that have all of the ship segments already in place.
3. Fill in ship segments in rows and columns that must have all of their remaining empty spaces filled in order to equal the corresponding number.

For the simplest Battleships, this is all that is needed to solve the puzzle. Take a look at the puzzle in Figure 1.

Throughout this chapter, columns of the grid will be referred to with uppercase letters A through J, while rows will be referred to with letters K through T. In this way, any square in the grid can be referenced with two letters: AK means the upper left square where column A crosses row K. In the example on the right, there are ship segments at CT, EM, and EQ, and water at IR.

To solve this puzzle, start with strategy 1: Fill in squares adjacent to the given ships. You know that the flat side of an end of a ship must have a ship segment next to it, so you can fill in DQ with a ship segment—it must be the other end of a destroyer because the row

Figure 1

	A	B	C	D	E	F	G	H	I	J	
K											0
L											1
M					■						5
N											1
O											2
P											1
Q				◗							2
R									≋		4
S											1
T			■								3
	1	2	2	2	5	1	0	2	1	4	

can only contain two ship segments. You can then fill in the spaces surrounding the destroyer with water. The ship segment at CT must be the middle part of a cruiser or one of the middle sections of the battleship. The ship must be horizontal (if it were vertical, it would extend below the bottom edge of the grid), so the squares to the left and right of CT (BT and DT) must have ship segments in them. Since row T can only have a total of three ship segments in it, BT-CT-DT must be a cruiser. The squares surrounding it can be filled in with water. The filled-in square at EM is also the middle section of a cruiser or one of the middle sections of the battleship. You don't know which yet, but you know that the four squares that touch a ship segment diagonally must be water, because ships never touch diagonally. Keep this in mind at all times for easier solving. Your grid should now look like Figure 2.

Now use strategy 2. Rows K, Q, and T, and columns D and G have all of their ship segments accounted for, so you can fill all the blank squares in those rows and columns with water. Your grid should now look like Figure 3.

Now look at EM. It must be part of a ship that goes vertically because DM is water, and the ship can no longer extend to the left. You could have figured this out using strategy 3 instead, since column E has only three blank spaces, all of which need to be filled with ship segments to reach the five needed. Since four segments in a row in column E are filled, that must be the battleship. Row R also has to have all of its empty spaces filled with ship segments. The left part, AR-BR must be a destroyer. The right part, HR and JR, must have ship segments in them, too. Don't make the mistake of filling them in with submarines—although they may be submarines, each one could also be the top half of a destroyer. To indicate that it's filled in with an unidentified ship segment, use a small dot in the middle of the square. Your grid should now look like Figure 4.

Whenever you fill in a ship segment, go back to strategy 1. Here, you can put water in FM and FO, and IS, too, since it touches a ship segment diagonally. And using strategy 2, you can put water in what's left of columns A and B and rows L and N, to get Figure 5.

It's time to use strategy 3 again. Column F must have a submarine in that empty space (it can't be some-

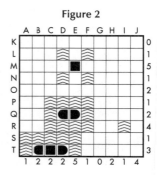

Figure 2

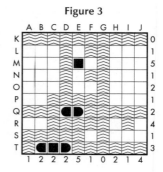

Figure 3

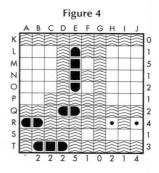

Figure 4

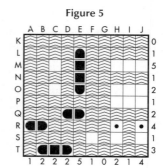

Figure 5

thing bigger because it's surrounded by water), and row M must have all four of its empty spaces filled with ship segments, making a submarine on the left and a cruiser on the right. This gives you Figure 6.

When you return to strategy 1 this time, you'll find it doesn't help, but strategy 2 does: You can fill in the blank spaces of columns C, H, and I and row S with water, since they already contain the required number of ship segments. Your grid now looks like Figure 7 .

The dots in row R are surrounded by water, so they must be submarines. And since you need two more ship segments in column J and have two spaces available, you can finish off the puzzle by filling those spaces with a destroyer. A quick double check verifies that you have all the required ships, so you're done (Figure 8).

The three basic strategies, though certainly important, will take you only so far. When you've reached a point at which the basic strategies provide no further help, the simplest advanced strategy is to try placing the largest ship that hasn't yet been located. If you haven't found where the battleship goes, try finding a spot for it. If the battleship is already in place, then look for spots for the cruisers. Here's an example (Figure 9).

First, of course, you should fill in what you can using the basic strategies. Your grid should now look like Figure 10.

Now, consider where the battleship can go. It must go in a row or column that has a four or higher. Only two qualify: row L and column E. It can't fit in row L, though—that row already contains a ship that can't be the battleship since there's only room for it to be a cruiser or destroyer, and the battleship can't go in the right part of the row since then there would be more than four

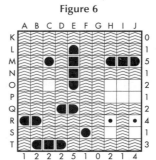

Figure 6

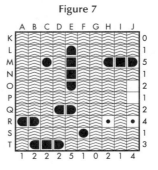

Figure 7

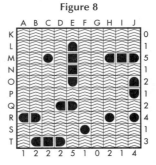

Figure 8

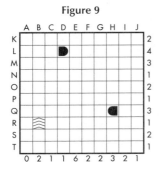

Figure 9

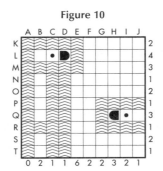

Figure 10

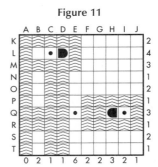

Figure 11

33

spaces filled by ships. So the battleship must go in column E. But where in the column? Its top can be at either EN, EO, EP, or EQ. You don't know which, but if you look at those four possibilities, you'll notice that in every case EQ is filled with a ship segment. So you can put a dot in EQ. Any time you put a dot in a square, you can immediately put water in the diagonally adjacent squares (since ships never touch diagonally), so fill in FP and FR with water. And look at row Q. It has its three ship segments, so the rest of it must be water—fill them in (Figure 11, page 33).

When you've filled in all the spaces surrounding a square that contains a dot, you can convert the dot to its proper ship segment. Here, square IQ must be the right end of a destroyer. Whenever you make a change using an advanced strategy, go back to you basic strategies to see if you can use them. Row R has only one empty space, and it has a one at the end of it, so that empty square must be filled with a ship segment. Since you don't yet know what type it is, put a dot in it. That dot gives you water in FS. Your grid should now look like Figure 12.

Now you'll need to think. Consider the four places the battleship can go. The first is EN-EO-EP-EQ. That's not possible because to put it there, ER would have to contain water, but it doesn't. The next possibility is EO-EP-EQ-ER. It fits, but putting it there would require water in EN and ES, leaving only one more blank space in column E, and two are needed to bring the total number of ship segments to six. So that possibility is out, too. The next possibility, EP-EQ-ER-ES, has the same problem—EO and ET would need to be water, leaving only one blank space (at EN), when two are needed to bring the total to six. So the last possibility, with the battleship at EQ-ER-ES-ET, must be correct; fill it in. That allows you to put water at EP and FT (Figure 13).

Now go back to the basic strategies. Fill in square BP with a dot (remember not to assume it's a submarine—it could extend upward!), and EN-EO with a destroyer. This puts water at FM, FN, and FO (Figure 14).

Continue using the basic strategies. Column F must contain a destroyer at FK-FL, and water must go in GK, GL, and GM. Now look at row M. HM-IM-JM must be a cruiser. This puts water in HL, IL, JL, GN, HN, IN, and JN. You can also fill in BN, IK, IO, IS, IT, JK, JO, JS, JT, BT, GT, and HT with water, giving you Figure 15.

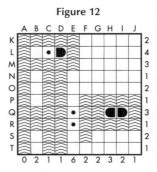

Figure 12

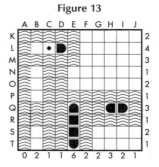

Figure 13

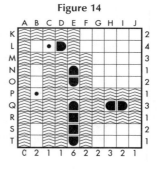

Figure 14

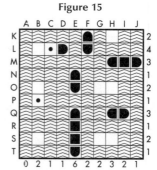

Figure 15

You can complete the puzzle with the basic strategies. Finish rows K and L first, and then columns B, G, and H. When you're done, your solution should look like Figure 16.

This example illustrates how a typical Battleships puzzle of medium difficulty can be solved. You start with the three basic strategies, then use some logical thinking to break through to the next step, and finish by again using the basic strategies. More difficult puzzles require more of these thought steps (Figure 17).

Using the basic strategies, you can get to the point shown in Figure 18.

Now try the advanced strategy of finding where the biggest remaining ship goes. In this case, the biggest ship not yet placed is the battleship. It can only go in column I (the only row or column with a four or higher), at either IK-IL-IM-IN or IL-IM-IN-IO. In both cases, IL, IM, and IN have ship segments in them, so you can fill those in. You can also put water in IT, since the battleship in the top of column I will use up all four allotted ship segments (Figure 19).

As always, after using an advanced strategy, you should reapply the basic strategies. You'll find you can put water in all the empty spaces of rows L and N, as well as in HK, HM, HO, JK, JM, and JO since they're diagonally adjacent to ship segments (Figure 20).

This is as far as you'll get with the basic strategies. It's time to try advanced strategy again. You know roughly where the battleship goes (somewhere at the top of column I); consider now where the cruisers can go. Only rows and columns with a three or higher are possibilities. You can rule out column I (since the battleship accounts for all four segments there), row M (since, after

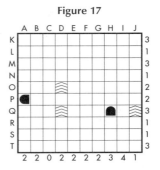

Figure 16

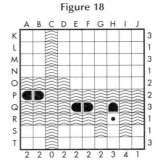

Figure 17

Figure 18

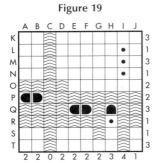

Figure 19

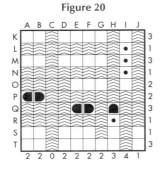

Figure 20

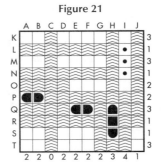

Figure 21

the component of the battleship is taken into account, there are only two more ship segments in that row), and row Q (which already has its three ship segments). That leaves column H, row K, and row T as possibilities. Two of those three must contain cruisers. If a cruiser goes in row K, it can only fit in the center section of four consecutive white squares. No matter where a cruiser fits in those four squares, square FK will have a ship segment in it. Similarly, if a cruiser goes in row T, it can only fit in the center section of five consecutive white squares. No matter where it fits in those five squares, square FT will have a ship segment in it. Since column F already contains one ship segment (FQ), the two cruisers can't go in both rows K and T at the same time, or else column F would have one too many ship segments in it. So one of the cruisers must be located in column H (and the other in either row K or row T). Column H can have only three ship segments in it, so the cruiser must be a part of what's already there. Fill it in with the surrounding water (Figure 21, page 35).

Now back to the basic strategies. Fill in water in the remaining spaces of row S; then it's clear that JT is a submarine (Figure 22).

Bingo! You now know the cruiser can't go in row T, since there's already a submarine in it, leaving only two remaining ship segments. So the cruiser must be in row K. You don't know its exact location; there are two possibilities, but in either case EK and FK must contain ship segments, and AK, BK, and IK must contain water, since all three ship segments in that row will be used up by the cruiser (Figure 23).

Back to the basic strategies. The battleship location has been determined in column I. You can fill the empty spaces in columns E and F with water, making GO a submarine (Figure 24).

Basic strategies still haven't finished off the puzzle. So again, look for a place for the largest remaining ship. You need one more destroyer. Row K is out—it's reserved for the cruiser. There are only two places left on the board with two adjacent white spaces: AM-BM and AT-BT. If the ship went in AM-BM, then AT and BT would contain water, leaving row T with at most two ship segments in it, which isn't enough. So the destroyer must instead be at AT-BT (Figure 25).

Figure 22

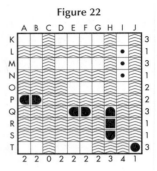

Figure 23

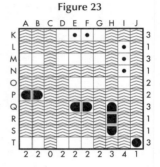

Figure 24

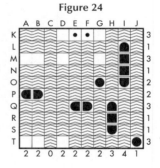

Figure 25

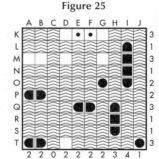

And now, at last, you can finish the puzzle with the basic strategies (Figure 26).

By now, you should know enough to get through all but the toughest of Battleships puzzles. Further advancement requires practice and more advanced strategies. Take a look at the next puzzle (Figure 27).

After using the basic strategies, the puzzle should look like Figure 28.

The biggest ship not yet placed is the battleship. Where can it go? Plenty of places: It could fit in one place in row N, one place in column B, or in any of four places in column J. You probably don't want to try that many possibilities. It's time for a different strategy: Look around the board for rows and columns that are almost determined. In particular, look for rows and columns in which the number of ship segments left to place is one less than the number of empty spaces. In this puzzle, row N needs four ship segments and has only five empty spaces. Row O needs three ship segments in the four remaining empty spaces. You'll find a similar condition in row Q, but for this puzzle you should concentrate on rows N and O. Consider square CN. If it's filled with a ship segment, then both BO and DO would have to contain water (since they're diagonally adjacent to CN). But that would leave only two empty spaces in row O for three ship segments—an impossibility! So CN can't contain a ship segment; fill it in with water. After filling CN with water, the basic strategies will take you a long way (Figure 29).

Now you go back to the first advanced strategy: Where can the biggest remaining ship go? In this case, you still need to place two destroyers. You can fit one of them in column C and the other in row K. They can't go anywhere else, so that's where they must be. The destroyer in row K must go at FK-GK, so CK is water, leaving CS-CT for the other destroyer (Figure 30).

From here, you just need to make the dot at CL a submarine and fill the blank squares with water, and you're done (Figure 31, page 38).

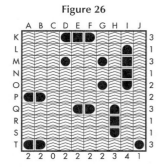

Figure 26

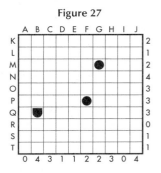

Figure 27

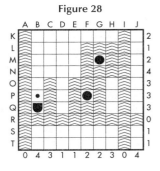

Figure 28

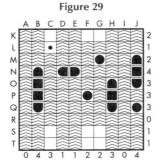

Figure 29

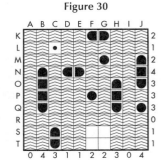

Figure 30

It's time for a toughie (Figure 32).

By now, the basic strategies should be second nature to you; applying them, your grid should look like Figure 33.

Now you'll need some deep thought. Where can the battleship go? Only in row M or row N. But you can be even more specific than that. It can't go at BM-CM-DM-EM because then AN, BN, CN, DN, EN, and FN would contain water, not leaving enough spaces for four ship segments in row N. Similarly, it can't go at BN-CN-DN-EN, because then row M would be impossible. So either the battleship goes at ABCD in one of these rows (M or N) with F and HIJ occupied in the other *or* it goes at CDEF in one of these rows with A and HIJ occupied in the other. In either case, the one at the bottom of column A is filled in row M or N, as is the one of column D and the one of column I. So you can put water in all the empty spaces in columns A, D, and I other than those in rows M and N (Figure 34).

Back to the basic strategies—they'll bring you to Figure 35.

You already know the battleship and one of the cruisers will go somewhere in rows M and N. Where will the other cruiser go? The only possibility is column B. Row Q and column E can be ruled out for obvious reasons. Columns C, H, and J are out because, as discussed above, at least one square in each of those columns will be part of a horizontal ship in row M or N. The cruiser in column B will account for all three hits in the column, so the battleship must go at CDEF of either row M or N, and either AM or AN must be a submarine. You can now place the cruiser in column B. Since it must include BP, its top is at BN, BO, or BP. If it were at BN or

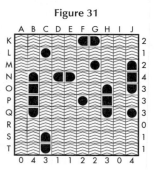

Figure 31

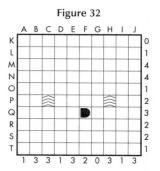

Figure 32

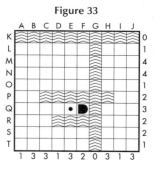

Figure 33

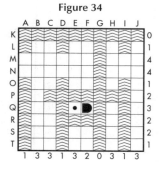

Figure 34

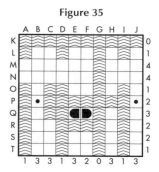

Figure 35

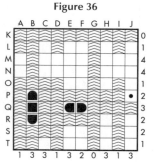

Figure 36

BO, then both AN and CN would contain water, making rows M and N impossible to finish, so the top of the cruiser must be at BP. Placing the cruiser at BP-BQ-BR and—of course—applying the basic startegies, yields Figure 36 (page 38).

Now look at column C. Three of those four squares must have ship segments. The battleship fits horizontally into either row M or N, taking up one of those three spaces. If it went in row M, then CL and CN would both contain water, making column C impossible. So the battleship goes at CN-DN-EN-FN. With basic strategies, you'll get Figure 37.

Check out the submarines—they've all been placed. That means the dot at JP can't be a submarine, so it must be part of a destroyer. And that gives you enough information to finish the puzzle (Figure 38).

One more puzzle (Figure 39) and then you're on your own to discover new, more advanced strategies.

Basic strategies don't help much (Figure 40).

Our advanced strategies don't help much either. The battleship can go in a number of places, and none of the rows or columns are within one of being filled. Sometimes solving the really hard puzzle requires trial and error.

The battleship can go in two places in column G and in six places in column I. Try them until one works. As soon as one works you can stop, because all Battleships have unique answers. Try the first of two locations in column G, namely GP-GQ-GR-GS. After surrounding the battleship with water, and completing column G with water, the next step is to complete column H with a cruiser at HL-HM-HN and complete column F with a ship segment at LF. But wait! Now row L has two ship

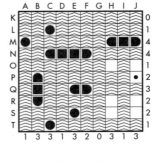

Figure 37

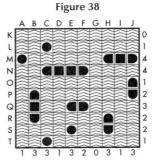

Figure 38

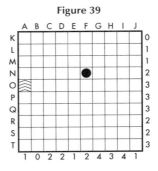

Figure 39

Figure 40

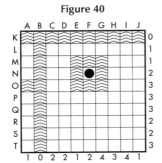

Figure 41

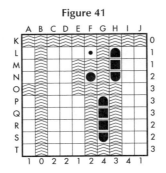

Figure 42

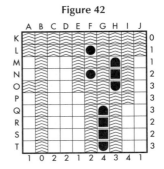

segments (Figure 41, page 39), which is one too many, so the battleship doesn't go at GP-GQ-GR-GS.

Moving on, try the battleship at the bottom of column G. Surround the ship with water and complete column F with a ship segment at FL and complete column G with water at GL. Now look at row L. Make the ship segment a submarine and complete the row with water. Now complete column H with a cruiser at HM-HN-HO and surround it with water. This leaves column I with four consecutive spaces that need to be filled, but the battleship can't go there since it's already in column G (Figure 42, page 39).

You now know the battleship is in column I. Try placing it next to the top, at IL-IM-IN-IO. (It can't start at IK since row K has no ship segments.) Surround the ship with water, and complete column I with water. Complete rows L, M, and N with water, and complete row O with a destroyer at CO-DO. Fill in the water surrounding the destroyer and complete row P with a submarine at AP and a destroyer at FP-GP. Surround that destroyer with water, and complete columns A and F with water. Now row Q must have a destroyer at CQ-DQ and a submarine at JQ. Surround the destroyer with water and complete columns C, D, and J with water. At last, there is an impossibility. Row R must have another destroyer in it, but there are none left. Also, columns G and H must both have cruisers in them adjacent to each other (Figure 43).

Onward you go, to IM-IN-IO-IP. Start by surrounding the battleship with water and completing its column with water. Next, complete column H with a cruiser at HR-HS-HT and surround it with water. This makes column G impossible (Figure 44).

Next up is IN-IO-IP-IQ. Start by surrounding the battleship with water and completing its column with water. Next, complete column H with a submarine at HL and a destroyer at HS-HT. Complete row L with water and surround the destroyer with water and column G becomes impossible (Figure 45).

Just three more possibilities. At this point you may start worrying that none of these three will work and that you'll have to go back and redo everything you've done so far to find your mistake. That's the wrong way to think. Have confidence! Keep working.

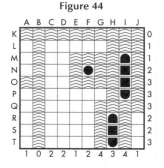

Figure 43

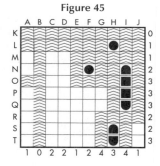

Figure 44

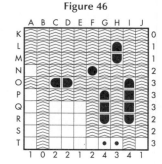

Figure 45

Figure 46

Moving down one more spot yields IO-IP-IQ-IR. As usual, surround the battleship with water and complete its column with water. Then complete column H with a destroyer at HL-ML and a ship segment at HT. Complete rows L and M with water and fill in water at GS (since it's diagonally adjacent to HT). Complete column G with a cruiser at GP-GQ-GR and a ship segment at GT, and surround the cruiser with water. Row O can be completed with a destroyer at CO-DO, and the water surrounding it can be filled in. Now both AN and AP must have ship segments to complete rows N and P, but column A can only have one ship segment in it, so it's yet another impossibility (Figure 46, page 40).

The next possibility is IP-IQ-IR-IS. This one doesn't last long at all. After surrounding the battleship with water and completing its column, there's an impossibility in row O (Figure 47).

So you are left with only one possibility, namely IQ-IR-IS-IT. It had better work! Basic strategies don't take you too far (Figure 48).

Don't be discouraged, though. You've made it this far. You'll sink this fleet yet! Move on to advanced strategy. Where can the longest not-yet-placed ship go? The cruisers can only go in column G, column H, or row P. If it went in row P though, row O would be impossible. Here's why: If the cruiser were at CP-DP-EP or at DP-EP-FP, then CO and DO would have to be water, leaving too few empty spaces in row O. If the cruiser were at EP-FP-GP, then DO and HO would have to be water, again leaving too few empty spaces in row O. Since those are the only three places where the cruiser can go in row P, it must not go.there. That leaves you only two places for the two cruisers, so they must go in those places:

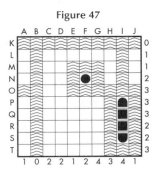

Figure 47

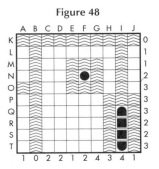

Figure 48

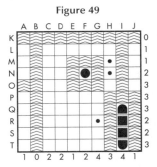

Figure 49

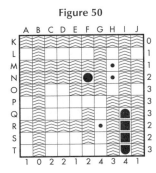

Figure 50

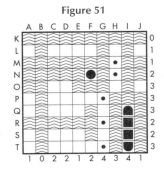

Figure 51

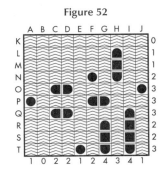

Figure 52

columns G and H. You don't know exactly where, but you do know that GR must contain a ship segment, as well as both HM and HN (Figure 49, page 41).

Using basic strategies now, you get Figure 50 (page 41).

Now, if GP were empty, then column G would need a battleship to fill it. But you've already used the battleship, so GP must have a ship segment. Similarly, GT can't be empty or else column G would need a battleship, so it too has a ship segment (Figure 51, page 41).

From here you can use basic strategies (starting off with water in HO since it's diagonally adjacent to GP, which has a ship segment in it) to finish up (Figure 52, page 41).

So there you have it. There are plenty of other strategies to use, depending on the puzzle. For example, if all the submarines are already in place, then every remaining ship segment must be a part of a longer ship, and if there's a column with a one that crosses a row with a one then it must contain water, since if it contained a ship, it would be a fifth submarine. Similarly, if three submarines are in place and there's a row with a two that has both adjacent rows filled with water, then you know the row with the two has to be a destroyer, not two submarines, since only one submarine is left to place. And then there's the case when ... well, you get the idea. Part of the fun is discovering new strategies.

And the best way to develop new strategies is to solve lots of puzzles.

1

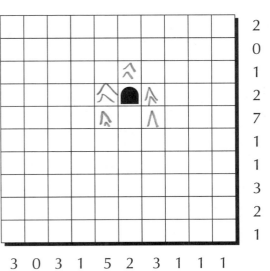

2

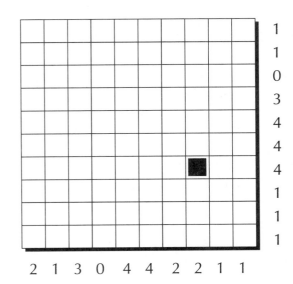

Battleship
Cruisers
Destroyers
Submarines

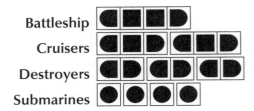

3

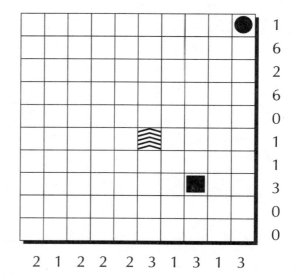

Battleship
Cruisers
Destroyers
Submarines

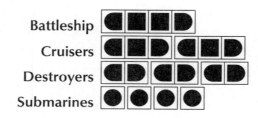

4

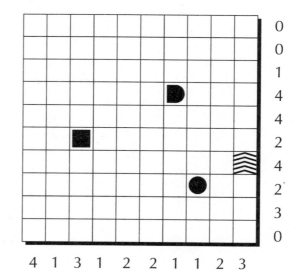

5

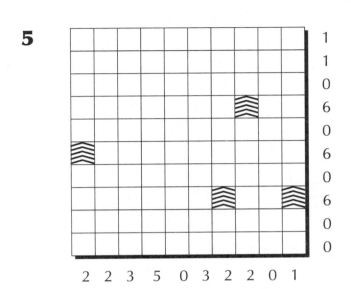

Row clues (top to bottom): 1 1 0 6 0 6 0 6 0 0 0

Column clues (left to right): 2 2 3 5 0 3 2 2 0 1

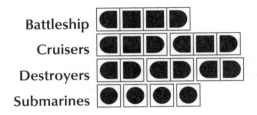

Battleship

Cruisers

Destroyers

Submarines

6

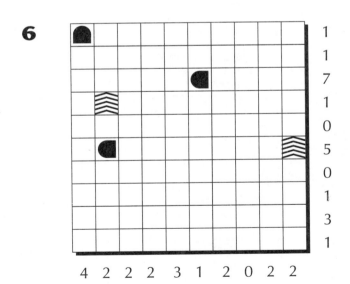

Row clues (top to bottom): 1 1 7 1 0 5 0 1 3 1

Column clues (left to right): 4 2 2 2 3 1 2 0 2 2

7

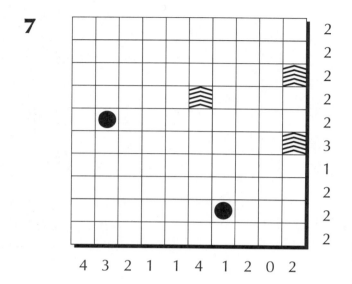

Battleship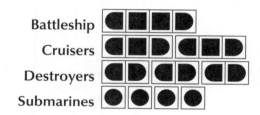
Cruisers
Destroyers
Submarines

8

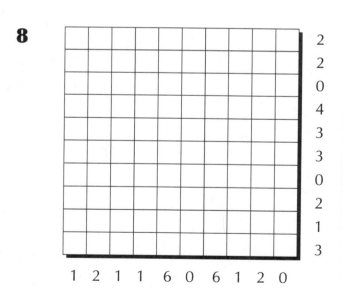

9

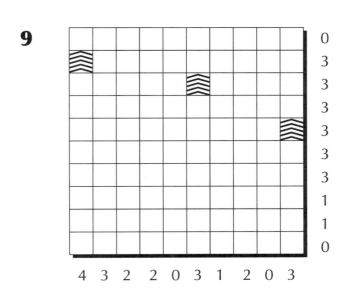

0
3
3
3
3
3
3
1
1
0

4 3 2 2 0 3 1 2 0 3

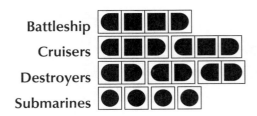

Battleship
Cruisers
Destroyers
Submarines

10

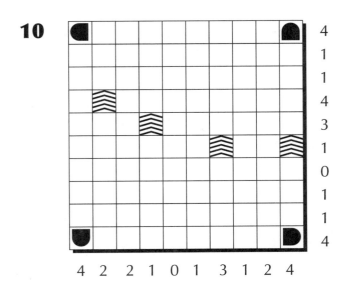

4
1
1
4
3
1
0
1
1
4

4 2 2 1 0 1 3 1 2 4

11

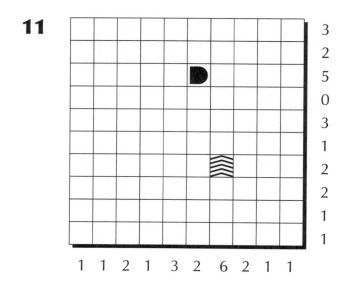

3
2
5
0
3
1
2
2
1
1

1 1 2 1 3 2 6 2 1 1

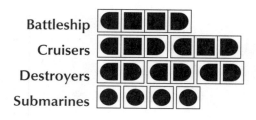

Battleship
Cruisers
Destroyers
Submarines

12

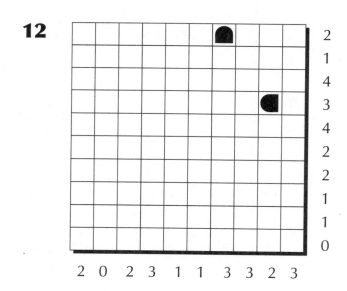

2
1
4
3
4
2
2
1
1
0

2 0 2 3 1 1 3 3 2 3

48

TRICKY MAZES

GENERAL INSTRUCTIONS

Where no specific instructions are given, find the route from A to B. One way to solve them is to start at B and color in all the blind alleys until you have the clear route.

Solutions—Pages 220-224

A Find a route from A to B that passes no more than four dots.

1

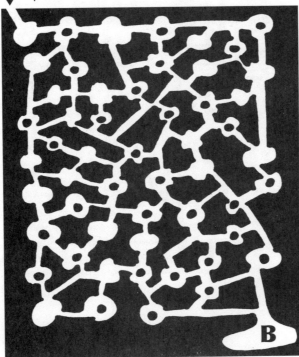

2

A
▼

▼
B

3

4

Draw a continuous line from A to B that passes through every one of the diamonds and none of the circles. The line may pass through each diamond once only.

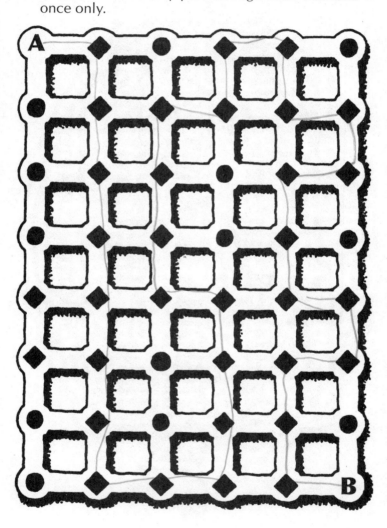

5

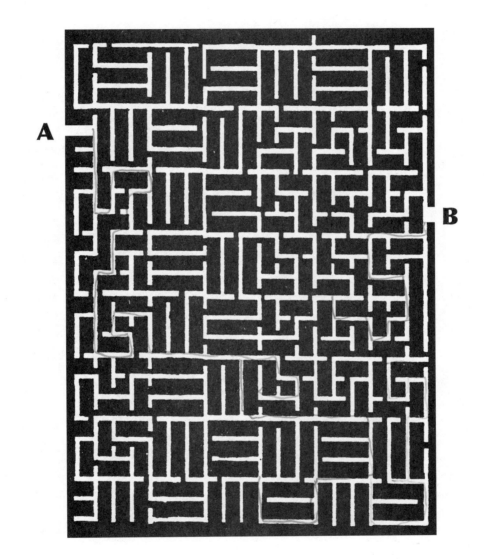

A

B

6

Which of the entrances at the bottom
leads to the exit at the top?

7

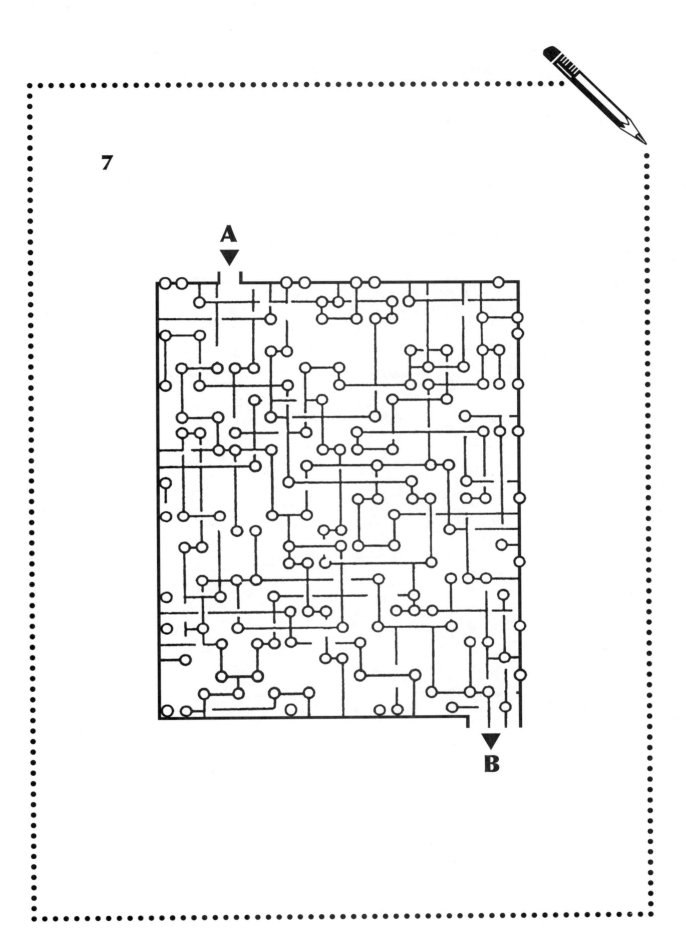

8

9

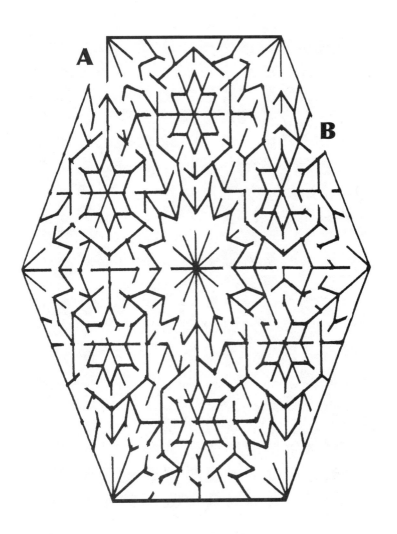

A B

10

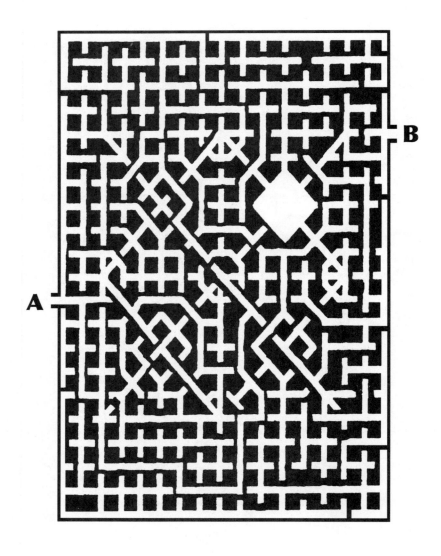

11

Find a route from A to B
that avoids C and D.

13

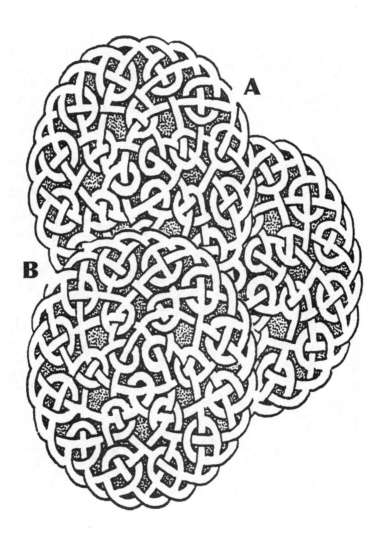

14

15

A

B

16

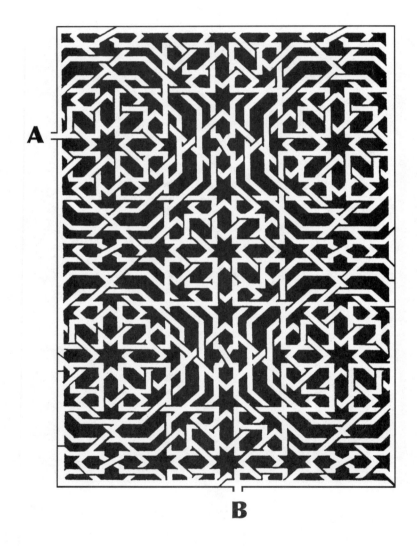

17

18

A

B

WHODUNITS

DR. J. L. QUICKSOLVE

Dr. Jeffrey Lynn Quicksolve, professor of criminology, retired from the police force as a detective at a very young age. Now he works with various police agencies and private detectives as a consultant when he isn't teaching at the university.

He certainly knows his business, solving crimes. Many people are amazed at how he solves so many crimes so quickly. He says, "The more you know about people and the world we live in, the easier it is to solve a problem."

His son, Junior, enjoys learning too, and he solves a few mysteries himself.

Read, listen, think carefully, and you can solve these crimes too!

Solutions—Pages 228-229

MURDER BETWEEN FRIENDS

The apartment building was an old house near the university. It had been divided into four apartments. The owner of the building, Gracious Host, lived in a large apartment downstairs. She rented out the three apartments upstairs. Dr. J. L. Quicksolve had heard the call over the police radio and arrived before the officers.

Gracious described her tenants to Dr. Quicksolve. She said Tweeter Woofer was a young "hippie type" who sometimes played her music too loudly. "I told her, one more complaint and she would be out on the street." Baby Blossom was hearing impaired, but "she reads lips." Terry Cloth was dead.

Gracious said she was sure only her three tenants were in the building when she heard the shots and discovered the body.

The hall was quiet when Dr. Quicksolve walked upstairs. The woman in the bathrobe lay against the wall, as if she were taking a nap. The three red stains told him the nap would last forever.

Dr. Quicksolve heard music in the back of the apartment and smelled burning incense when Tweeter Woofer opened her apartment door to let him enter. Miss Woofer was shocked when he explained what had happened. As they stood inside the door, she said, "This is so upsetting. Who would shoot Terry?" She said she did not hear anything and did not see anything.

Dr. Quicksolve knocked quietly on Baby Blossom's door. She and her dog , a yellow Labrador, came to the door. He explained what happened. "I was a little afraid to open the door because I thought I heard shots," she said. "I guess I was right."

When Dr. Quicksolve went back downstairs, the policemen had arrived. "I have a good suspect," he told them.

Which woman did he suspect?

INHERITANCE

"A small turtle sundae, please," Dr. J. L. Quicksolve told the waitress. He was the last to order. His friend, Fred Fraudstop, had invited Dr. Quicksolve and his son, Junior, for an ice cream treat to celebrate Fred's move into town. Fred ordered a chocolate-marshmallow sundae, and Junior ordered a "freight train"—two banana splits in separate glass bowls pulled by a glass train engine. If you ate the whole thing, you got to keep the glass engine. Junior had five of them at home.

"That reminds me of a railroad tycoon who died recently. He was an only child and a bachelor who kept to himself, though he loved to travel through the West when he was younger. Studying the Old West was a hobby of his. We had to hunt for his next-of-kin," Fred said as Junior's ice cream was brought out by two waitresses wearing conductor's caps and red bandannas.

"Did you find anybody?" Junior asked, reaching for his spoon.

"They found us, " Fred said, "which wasn't surprising considering the money they stood to inherit. I've narrowed it down to two people. The rest are obviously just pretending to be relatives, hoping to get the money."

"Who are they?" Junior asked.

"One is a niece from Chicago, and the other is a cousin from North Dakota. They're the only ones who don't have a previous record of fraud of some sort or another. I still have to check out their claims, though. Would you like to talk to them with me?" he asked Dr. Quicksolve.

"Sure; it sounds interesting," the detective answered. "Let's start with the one from North Dakota."

Why did Dr. Quicksolve want to talk to the relative from North Dakota?

STRIKEOUT

Dr. J. L. Quicksolve and Junior were meeting Fred Fraudstop for lunch. Fred said he had to stop and question a man about a burglary at the Strikeout Sportscard Shop. Dr. Quicksolve decided to go with him because Junior was a baseball card collector and would be interested in the shop, not to mention Quicksolve's curiosity about the burglary.

"We were broken into overnight," Homer Hitter, the shop owner, told them. "They took a bunch of cards, but mostly money," he said, showing them the back door that had been jimmied open and the empty moneybox. "We close late, so I usually take the money to the bank in the morning," he said.

"Did you lock up last night?" Dr. Quicksolve asked him. Junior was looking at a display of Mickey Mantle cards. He showed his dad the 1953 rookie card that had a price of $300 on it. "Save your money," Dr. Quicksolve said.

"No, my clerk, Art Dunn, closed up last night. He always closes up. He bolts the back door and goes out the front. I let him have his own key. I don't think he would do anything like this." Then he noticed Junior looking at the cards. "You like Mickey Mantle?" he asked Junior. He reached below the counter and brought out a card that showed Mantle standing at the left side of the plate as if he were waiting for a pitch. "Without all those injuries he would have been the Home Run King."

"What do you think of the Strikeout Sportscard Shop?" Fred asked Junior as they walked out onto the sidewalk.

"I don't think I'd buy anything from that guy," Junior said, "and you probably should doubt what he tells you about the robbery."

Why does Junior mistrust Homer?

CODDLED COED

Three college coeds rented the house next to Dr. J. L. Quicksolve. Brenda Broadcloth and Cherry Ripple, two of them, ran up to Dr. Quicksolve in front of his house just as he was saying goodbye to Sergeant Rebekah Shurshot. Brenda said they had been robbed.

    The three roommates had shopped together. They had bought their groceries, including cod for that night's dinner because Holly Mackeral loved fish. Brenda chose asparagus for the vegetable, and Cherry chose vanilla ice cream for dessert.

"I had the money, but I put it back in the cookie jar when we got home," Brenda said. "Then I went upstairs to call my boyfriend. That was about three o'clock."

"I fed the cat and went out to work in the backyard. I decided to get bananas for the ice cream," Cherry said, "so I went to the cookie jar for the money around four-thirty. The money was gone. I guess someone came into the house and took it."

Holly came walking up with their dog Furball on a leash. Brenda told her about the robbery. Sergeant Shurshot asked Holly what she did after they came back from shopping.

"I unwrapped the fish and put it on the counter to thaw a little. Then I went to the basement to read. Shortly after four I put the fish in the oven and took the dog for a walk. I didn't see anybody," she said.

"Will you check the cookie jar for fingerprints?" Brenda asked Sergeant Shurshot.

"I don't think that will be necessary. This was an inside job," Sergeant Shurshot responded.

What did Sergeant Shurshot mean?

TELEPHONE RING

Dr. J. L. Quicksolve and Junior sat in the airport waiting for Captain Reelumin's plane to arrive. Junior liked to watch the people going by. He liked to guess things about who they might be and where they were going.

Dr. Quicksolve watched people make phone calls at a round table filled with telephones, each with its tiny "booth," small dividers that separated the phones. He noticed one man kept a phone to his ear with one hand. He held a pencil with the other hand, as if he was getting instructions or directions, but he had not written anything down. A man in a jacket took the phone in the adjoining booth. He took a card out of his pocket that he looked at as he spoke into the telephone. The first man finally wrote something down.

"See those two men?" Dr. Quicksolve asked his son.

"Yes," Junior said, noticing that his father was staring at the two men by the phones. The one in the jacket walked away, and the other man suddenly hung up his phone. Then he held it to his ear again and began making another call, talking into the phone as he looked down at his notepad.

"Get that man," Dr. Quicksolve said quietly, pointing to the man in the jacket who had just walked by them. Dr. Quicksolve walked up behind the man on the telephone and looked over his shoulder.

What did he expect to see?

BEN BOINKT

Dr. J. L. Quicksolve walked in the open door, passed a man lying on the couch with an icepack on his head, and proceeded into the dining room, following the voices he heard.

"That's Ben Boinkt out there on the couch," Officer Longarm said to Dr. Quicksolve.

A woman sat at the table. She had so much makeup on, Dr. Quicksolve wondered what she really looked like. Then, through the doorway that led to the kitchen, he saw the body of a woman.

"Mrs. Boinkt is dead," Officer Longarm said, answering the unspoken question. "This is Miss Glenda Cheatenheart," he said, indicating the woman at the table. "She lives next door. She found the Boinkts lying on the floor in the kitchen."

Dr. Quicksolve looked into the kitchen, where the body lay. The back door lock had been broken, and the door was open.

"I heard the crash of the door in the kitchen," Mr. Boinkt said as he stood in the dining-room doorway holding the icepack to his head. Then I heard my wife falling down when the thugs hit her from behind. There were two of them. They never said a word and they wore masks. I turned to run, but they caught me from behind and knocked me out cold. They went upstairs to the wall safe in our bedroom. They took my wife's jewels and about $200 in cash."

"I saw what happened in the kitchen through my window next door," Glenda said. "I called the police right away and ran over here with my gun, but they were gone."

Dr. Quicksolve looked at Ben and Glenda. He walked up the stairs without saying a word. When he came down, he said, "I think Mr. Boinkt needs his head examined."

What did he mean?

SOCKS

Bobby Socks looked menacing sitting in Mr. Paddlebottom's office when Junior and Kimberly Kay walked into the principal's office. Bobby wore his jeans tucked into baseball socks just below his knees. Most kids thought it looked funny. That suited Bobby fine because he used every excuse he could think of to start a fight. He had beaten up almost every boy in school at one time or another over some imagined insult. Junior was one of the few boys Bobby would not mess with, though. Junior figured Bobby was afraid to pick on the son of the famous Dr. J. L. Quicksolve. It was as if he had something to hide and was afraid Junior would figure it out. He was right.

Kimberly's new skateboard had been stolen from her garage yesterday afternoon. She was sure she had seen Bobby in his baseball uniform pushing her bike away. Mr. Paddlebottom wanted to talk to Kimberly and Bobby before he called Bobby's parents or the police. Kimberly had asked Junior to go with her to the office for moral support.

"It was seven o'clock," Kimberly said when the principal asked her the time she thought she saw Bobby taking her bike. "I was looking out the front door for my girlfriend. Her dad was going to take us shopping," she said.

"I was playing baseball in the park at seven," Bobby said. "We were playing those bums from Jackson. We were just getting our last bats. We were ahead five to nothing when I hit my second home run of the game. Then I walked home with Michael Thomas. You can ask him."

"You can't believe Bobby's story, Mr. Paddlebottom," Junior said to the principal.

Why doesn't Junior believe Bobby is telling the truth?

WORD SEARCHES 1

GENERAL INSTRUCTIONS

Welcome to the wonderful world of word searches. (Say *that* three times fast!) Sure, words are used primarily to communicate, but let's face it—they're a lot of fun to play with, too. And there are lots of ways to play with them.

A word search puzzle is like a game of hide-and-seek. We hide the words—you go seek them. If you've never solved a word search, no problem. We'll explain all the rules shortly. If you have done word searches, keep reading. You'll learn about the twists we've added for some extra fun.

A word search puzzle is made up of two main parts: a grid and a word list. The usually rectangular-shaped grid is filled with what looks to be a meaningless jumble of letters. Actually, that jumble hides all the words and phrases given in the word list, which appears on the same page.

Hidden words and phrases always go in a straight line, but may run horizontally, vertically, or diagonally. Horizontal words (words that go across) may run forward or backward. Vertical words may go down or up. Diagonal words (top left to lower right, or top right to lower left) may run up or down along their angle. So words may run in any of eight possible directions. Also, be aware that the same letter may be used more than once when words cross it in two or more directions. Furthermore, ignore all punctuation and spaces in the word list when searching in the grid. For example, "That's all,

Solutions—Pages 230-238

folks!" would appear in the grid, in some direction, as THATSALLFOLKS. If all that sounds confusing, don't worry—it won't be for long. All it takes is a little practice.

You can tackle a word search in many ways. Some solvers start by searching for the across words. Others look for the long words first or words containing less common letters such as Q, Z, X, or J. Still others begin at the top of the word list and methodically work their way to the bottom. Whatever works for you is fine.

The same holds true for marking the grid. You can loop the hidden words, draw a straight line through them, or circle each individual letter. Whatever you choose, we recommend you cross off the words on the word list as you find them in the grid.

Each of these puzzles has a different theme and about the same level of difficulty. All but three of the grids are in the shape of a rectangle with 11 letters across and 15 letters down. (That's useful to know. If a word or phrase is more than 11 letters long, it is too long to go across or diagonally and so it must run vertically.) Each word list, except one, has 20 words or phrases.

Each puzzle contains a hidden message! After you've found all the words in a grid, read the unused letters left to right, row by row, from top to bottom and you'll discover that they spell out a hidden message relating to the puzzle's theme. (There's no punctuation, so you'll have to figure that out, too.) Hidden messages contain silly sayings, puns, riddles, amazing facts, quotations, definitions, or interesting observations.

Another puzzle-within-a-puzzle may be the theme itself. Sometimes the puzzle's title will make the theme obvious. Other times, you'll need to use a little imagination to see what the title means.

There are other added twists. A few grids have shapes related to their themes. One contains numbers. And some puzzles, when completed, display specially designed loop patterns.

If you draw loops (and most solvers do), make sure the loop contains only the letters in the word you've found and no other letters. Otherwise, you'll end up missing letters from the hidden message.

+ 11 = verticaly

DRIVES A DICE ENGAGE MIND BEFORE
PUTTING MOOTHI N GEAR

GETTING STARTED

DRIVES A DICE ENGA GEMIND
BEFORE
PUTTING
MOUTING
EAR

```
D E C A R G Y A S T D
N R T Y O I F V E A R
S O S H D A F D O K V
O I C E A O R E E W
P D L T N G E A G A E
E M N G I H E R R D I
N N E E T D T M T E S
T D B T E F U O R E E
H P I U U P K A D P G
E H T P T R U I I B N
B D E T A E S E B R G
O M E B H K O U K E P
O T M A C I H P L A N
K E I I L N N G C T W
E A P H C T E K S H R
```

✓ AUDITION   ✓ PACK
✓ BE SEATED   ✓ PICK SIDES
✓ DEAL   PLAN
✓ EMBARK   ✓ SAY GRACE
✓ ENLIST   ✓ SKETCH
✓ GET READY   ✓ TAKE A DEEP BREATH
✓ GET UP   ✓ TEE OFF
✓ GO HIDE   ✓ THINK
✓ HIT THE ROAD   ✓ WAKE UP
✓ OPEN THE BOOK   ✓ WARM UP

+11 = vertical

CHECK THIS OUT

If you play chess, alot are y u a chess nut

```
I F B Y N G O
D R A O B A W U P
L A E B M E T A M
A N T B I S H O P
Y K I Y C T A K E
H T H F E S C S A
L W I M O V E
O S L T A
R C E N Y
C H E C K
D E O C N
U R A U I
Q A L A C G H
E S B S N W H U T
K I N G N I L T S A C
```

✓BISHOP   ✓KING
✓BLACK   ✓KNIGHT
✓BOARD   ✓MATE
✓BOBBY FISCHER   ✓MOVE
✓CASTLING   ✓PAWN
✓CHECK   ✓QUEEN
✓CLOCK   ✓RANK
✓DRAW   ✓TAKE
✓GAMBIT   ✓WHITE

FATHER'S DAY

The best dad dy would win a popularity contest!

```
D F O R E F A T H E R
T A P O P C O R N S P
H T D E B R E A S G O
T H P O P A R T D E P
H E A O O W D P D L S
O R M Y P D W O O G I
P F U I L A D P L N C
O I W Y T D D O T O L
N G N P A R L O P L E
P U P O L E O S Y P
O R G O I U P H E D L
P E A P R T I P T D D
T Y O C O P O P L A R
O P N P T P E S D D F
T Y D D A D R A G U S
```

CRAWDAD
DADA
DADDY-LONGLEGS
DOODAD
FATHER FIGURE
FATHER TIME
FOREFATHER
HOP ON POP
LOLLIPOP
POP ART

POPCORN
POPEYE
POPGUN
POPLAR
POPPY
POPSICLE
POP-TART
POP-TOP
SODA POP
SUGAR DADDY

AT THE MALL

Tall Pauls always crawl on the wall at that small mall

```
T  R  U  O  C  D  O  O  F  T  A
L  L  P  A  A  E  S  W  O  R  B
A  U  R  L  S  R  A  W  E  A  S
S  T  A  R  B  U  C  K  S  P  C
S  R  H  A  T  W  C  A  L  A  O
Y  N  T  E  O  O  H  E  D  G  W
A  C  F  I  L  E  N  E  S  E  S
D  T  L  T  G  I  W  A  R  H  D
I  U  O  A  N  L  M  C  L  T  L
R  O  A  T  I  S  J  I  T  S  A
F  G  S  H  K  R  H  A  T  T  N
I  N  S  R  R  M  E  O  A  E  O
G  A  L  L  A  M  R  S  P  A  D
T  H  J  C  P  E  N  N  E  Y  C
L  L  N  O  R  D  S  T  R  O  M
```

ARCADE	MCDONALD'S
BROWSE	NORDSTROM
CARTS	PARKING LOT
CLAIRE'S	SEARS
FILENE'S	SHOP
FOOD COURT	STARBUCKS
FOOT LOCKER	STORE
HANG OUT	T.G.I. FRIDAY'S
J.C. PENNEY	THE GAP
J. CREW	THE LIMITED

X MARKS THE SPOT

a boxer put the mix of kix trix and rice chex in the ice box

```
X O B D N A S A B H B
O I O X E R A P E U A
S T S E L I F X E H T
P T T P H E A L L M T
H I O X E G O O E E L
I A N F O E K U N I E
N X R N T R D I O E A
X I E P X A H S H L X
E Y D N O C D X P O R
I X S C A M E I O H O
E A O M C R A V L X C
Y L X D O H E R Y O I
X A I X U N T G X F X
F G R H E S E I C E
B O X X I N E O H P M
```

AXLE	LOUIS XIV
BATTLE-AX	MEXICO
BOSTON RED SOX	OXYGEN
DEEP-SIX	PHOENIX
EXODUS	SANDBOX
FAX MACHINE	SPHINX
FOXHOLE	THE X-FILES
GALAXY	XEROX
HARPO MARX	X-RAY
HEXAGON	XYLOPHONE

THE SIMPSONS

```
D L E I F G N I R P S
T O D H E O S P A A R
Y E N R A B B C P E E
B A A U L I E M N S N
W A K H T O A S I E N
H M R B U R N S D J I
Y O A T G W U F N P K
H O B N O M L C E C S
C A A S K A I I L A R
T O P N N R G A S R U
A R P D E G U I O K O
R A E N A E L S N T M
C R L M G Y H C T I Y
S A N D O K O O D Y E
O S S R E H T I M S S
```

BARNEY	MAGGIE
BART	MARGE
DONUT	MR. BURNS
EDNA KRABAPPEL	NED FLANDERS
GRAMPA	NELSON
HOMER	OTTO
ITCHY	SCRATCHY
JIMBO	SEYMOUR SKINNER
KRUSTY	SMITHERS
LISA	SPRINGFIELD

CIRCLING THE BASES

```
        B  T  C
     A  E  H  E  A
     S  T  R  I  K  E  T
  E  E  Y  I  E  V  R  U  C
  H  O  I  U  P  N  R  E  M  O  H
  I  G  E  R  S  M  T  M  T  A  C  J  E
T  T  R  O  E  P  U  R  E  T  T  A  B  K  R
P  N  R  E  S  O  U  T  F  I  E  L  D  L  B
L  U  O  N  D  E  C  K  P  H  E  A  G  A  U
  B  E  E  L  I  R  D  F  O  U  L  C  B
  W  K  R  A  L  S  E  N  A  K  G
     E  O  I  F  S  R  I  S  F
     W  H  T  E  R  T  E
        H  C  A  O  C
           N  P  R
```

BACKSTOP	FOUL
BALK	HOMER
BASE HIT	NO-HITTER
"BATTER UP!"	ON DECK
BUNT	OUTFIELD
CATCHER	SLIDER
CHOKE UP	STRIKE
COACH	UMPIRE
CURVE	WILD PITCH
ERROR	WORLD SERIES

"IT'S ABOUT TIME!"

```
T R A E Y T H G I L I
M O O E N E H I S T L
H N E G D O C S M O A
S T H G I N T R O F I
S I M T T V A N A O D
A M L I U D W H O A N
L E B M N L L E G W U
A T H E I U A N G I S
R A L R B M T A I N B
M A C A N I I E N S P
C O H O U R G L A S S
L E N N D T I B S K H
O R E T A L D E E O P
C H R A H S T E C N U
K S S T O P W A T C H
```

ALARM CLOCK
BIG BEN
BIG HAND
CALENDAR
DIGITAL WATCH
EGG TIMER
EONS
FORTNIGHT
HOURGLASS
"IN A SEC!"

LATER
LIGHT-YEAR
MINUTE
MONTH
"NOT NOW!"
ON TIME
SOON
STOPWATCH
SUNDIAL
WEEK

AT THE MOVIES

```
O A D P O P C O R N T
T N N T O H A E M E O
N V A S I E S D K Y O
E U T D B A L C O N Y
E E S P A A I Y T S O
R S N M A T I N E E N
C I O T I N E T H O E
S T I C K Y F L O O R
P D S A H H H S R D A
K R S W I T G O O H T
Y A E L O N G L I N E
B D C V I L B D O T D
B O N M I Y F O S T P
O R O A A E B U T S G
L C C N C G W T E R S
```

BALCONY   POSTER
CANDY   PREVIEW
COMING SOON   RATED PG
CONCESSION STAND   SCREEEN
DOLBY   "SHHH!"
LOBBY   SODA
LONG LINE   SOLD OUT
MATINEE   STICKY FLOOR
ON A DATE   STUB
POP CORN   TICKET

SURFING THE WEB

```
S  M  W  H  S  E  N  I  J  A  G
R  E  T  T  E  L  N  I  A  H  C
I  S  A  R  L  T  R  S  V  H  B
E  S  N  R  E  Y  D  U  A  S  E
Y  A  A  R  C  A  N  T  E  L  W
E  G  N  C  T  H  R  R  O  N  E
I  E  I  P  R  O  F  I  L  E  D
T  B  C  D  O  O  M  E  S  A  I
W  O  E  M  O  D  E  M  O  S  W
E  A  N  A  G  R  E  L  T  N  D
B  R  I  U  H  A  P  T  O  S  L
S  D  L  F  J  U  E  G  M  I  R
I  A  N  L  E  E  O  M  A  A  O
T  I  O  B  U  L  C  M  I  S  W
E  M  A  N  N  E  E  R  C  S  L
```

CHAIN LETTER	PRODIGY
CHAT ROOM	PROFILE
E-MAIL	SCREEN NAME
INTERNET	SEARCH
JAVA	SIM CLUB
JUNO	UPLOAD
LOG ON	U.R.L.'S
MESSAGE BOARD	WEB SITE
MODEM	WORLD WIDE WEB
ONLINE	YAHOO

LIFE'S A PICNIC

```
B A D O S P O A P D I
L U C T N U I I C A M
A E N A N S S R D L C
N A T S A T F E U A N
K E E G T A I G R S R
E I K O O C M R E O A
T B S C F D O U O T W
O D A F I T T B I A H
S L B R S H L O L T C
E E C T B D C S H O I
C H I P S E E O O P W
U C N P T L C L I N D
K G C O O R E U E A N
S Y I C T R A S E K A
P A P E R P L A T E S
```

ANTS
BARBECUE
BLANKET
BUNS
BURGER
CARROT STICK
CATSUP
CHICKEN
CHIPS
COLE SLAW

COOKIE
COOLER
HOT DOG
PAPER PLATES
PICNIC BASKET
PIES
POTATO SALAD
RADIO
SANDWICH
SODA

PIECE A PIZZA

```
N O O O M A E F T
T T A N C H O V I E S
T E L A R A H O I W I T Y
O S U G A S L M I L N C E A
B U E M U S H R O O M I
R R R T R Y E O U R R
O C L H E G A E
C I L R A G P
C V A E T P R O
O O B A E L D U M I
L S T P T A T H B I S P
I W A A A N P A R M E S A N
S E U M T S A U S A G E E
M A C O S Y T A S H P
I E E T O N I O N
```

ANCHOVIES
BROCCOLI
CRUST
EGGPLANT
FETA
GARLIC
HAMBURGER
MEATBALL
MUSHROOM
OLIVE

ONION
OREGANO
PARMESAN
PEPPERONI
PESTO
ROMANO
SALT
SAUCE
SAUSAGE
TOMATO

? who puts this on pizza?!

✓ toe

95

MONOPOLY GAME

```
E  T  N  E  R  M  Y  P  O  N  B
O  S  K  R  O  W  R  E  T  A  W
S  E  U  P  O  O  L  Y  N  P  R
O  H  P  O  P  E  R  K  T  O  I
E  C  O  E  H  N  E  K  O  T  M
S  Y  R  R  O  R  A  R  E  N  K
L  T  X  A  T  Y  R  U  X  U  L
Y  I  A  M  E  L  A  E  D  D  A
A  N  A  F  L  T  I  E  I  R  W
S  U  T  J  R  C  L  N  C  E  D
E  M  T  S  H  I  R  N  E  A  R
R  M  T  A  L  A  O  M  N  T  A
D  O  N  O  T  P  A  S  S  G  O
I  C  L  C  C  G  D  I  T  Y  B
E  C  A  L  P  K  R  A  P  N  J
```

BANKER	LUXURY TAX
BOARDWALK	MONEY
CHANCE	PARK PLACE
COMMUNITY CHEST	PROPERTY
DICE	RAILROAD
DO NOT PASS GO	RENT
GAME	ROLL
HOTEL	SHORT LINE
HOUSE	TOKEN
JAIL	WATER WORKS

A BAND WE'D LIKE TO HEAR

```
B F L U G E L H O R N
M A R O U S I C A O I
S T N E L G N A I R T
B G X J M H E D U N P
I A A V O I R E R S E
A L S O L O C C I P N
L A O S C U N L G U N
L A N C D G T E U M Y
C Y A O T R F E A D W
H U R D Y G U R D Y H
I M P E M A A M E N I
M K O I P C N F D L S
E O S M A R I M B A T
S N G S N F F E L L L
O S E P I P G A B W E
```

ACCORDION   HURDY-GURDY
BAGPIPES   LUTE
BANJO   LYRE
BASS DRUM   MARACAS
CHIMES   MARIMBA
DULCIMER   PENNYWHISTLE
FIFE   PICCOLO
FLUGELHORN   SOPRANO SAX
GONG   TRIANGLE
HARP   TYMPANI

THINGS THAT SPIN

```
H  W  E  E  R  A  D  R  E  A  S
T  P  E  D  A  E  H  R  U  O  Y
R  I  B  N  R  N  C  G  I  R  N
A  G  S  V  O  O  E  N  P  O  N
E  U  I  R  O  R  C  R  A  O  W
E  S  R  E  N  F  O  E  T  D  A
H  T  F  N  E  P  S  A  R  G  G
T  O  O  A  E  D  B  O  R  N  E
M  R  A  L  L  I  M  D  N  I  W
V  I  L  P  E  S  L  W  D  V  L
S  E  I  T  D  L  K  R  L  L  E
R  P  I  N  I  A  Y  A  A  O  E
M  J  O  U  E  E  A  B  T  V  H
C  E  N  T  R  I  F  U  G  E  W
M  E  S  S  D  R  O  T  O  R  R
```

AUGER	RECORD
BALL	REVOLVING DOOR
BATON	ROTOR
CENTRIFUGE	SKATER
DANCER	STUNT PLANE
DERVISH	THE EARTH
DREIDEL	TOPS
DRYER	WHEEL
FRISBEE	WINDMILL ARM
PROPELLER	YOUR HEAD

CAMP SIGHTS

```
H Y A D S T N E R A P
O C R A M P K S O R N
R G S E A I S N D T S
S W I M H C H A G S R
E Y S O T C O O O A K
B C R S M O R E S N T
A I O Q E F T A U D U
C T R U N K S B S C O
K A R I N E H F U R S
R N A T R S E S P A T
I N N O O U E N I F H
D S I N N E T L D T G
I T B A H E I C O S I
N A A M R N P F I R L
G R C E G A T E M A N
```

ARCHERY	NAMETAG
ARTS AND CRAFTS	PARENT'S DAY
BUNK	RAIN
CABIN	SAILING
COUNSELOR	SHORT-SHEET
FROG	S'MORES
HIKE	SWIM
HORESEBACK RIDING	TAPS
"LIGHTS OUT!"	TENNIS
MOSQUITO	TRUNK

HINKY PINKY

A Hinky Pinky is a two-word rhyming phrase in which each word has the same number of syllables. A simple example is DAN RAN. In this case, just one letter—the first—changes from word to word. We think that more variety adds more fun, so in the list below, each word in the pair is spelled significantly different from the other.

```
Y E K R U T Y K R E J
S E I X H L I P E C S
K T O O F E W T S H S
F N W H A L E J A I L
D O G R S P O Q Z N E
S I A H T E S I W J T
H T A E O W U E E U Y
W O E M A S R L O R N
E M T X D G N T B E N
N N H Y U E E G A G E
K A O O A R H R E I P
O E L C E C P G T N Y
H C K P N I H Y I G N
W O E A E W R T K E A
S T O R E D O O R R W
```

ANY PENNY
BLUE SHOE
DRY TIE
HIGH FLY
HOT YACHT
INJURE GINGER
I SPY
JERKY TURKEY
LOU GREW
MEET PETE

NEAR PIER
OCEAN MOTION
OWN CONE
SHAQ'S WAX
STORE DOOR
TOO FEW
WEIGHED MAID
WHALE JAIL
WHO KNEW
WISE THAIS

WORDWORKS

GENERAL INSTRUCTIONS

In the games that follow, vocabulary fiends can find many hidden words in the designated word for each game. Use only words of four or more letters and no proper nouns.

Solutions—Pages 239-243

1 "GAMESTER"

Find up to 82 words in the playful noun above. A score of 40 deserves a red ribbon; 50, a blue one; and 60, the dictionary hall of fame!

(4 letters)

GAME
REST
MARE
GAME
MEET

(5 letters)

(6 letters)

(7 letters)

2 "FAVORITE"

Find at least 50 words in this shining example. Score 30 to be a tough contender; go for broke with 35; find 45, and you'll be favored in any word race!

(4 letters)   **(5 letters)**

3 "BETROTHAL"

There are 114 words concealed here. Finding 70 means you're a real word lover; 80, you're totally committed; and 90 or more gets the brass ring!

(4 letters)   **(5 letters)**   **(6 letters)**

(7 letters)

4 "DEVELOPMENT"

Seek out the 94 words concealed here. Get 60 words for a good foundation; 70, and you've done the framework; 80 or more, and you're a master wordsmith!

(4 letters)

(5 letters)

(6 letters)

(7 letters)

(8 letters)

(9 letters)

5 "EXEMPLARY"

Search for the 68 words hidden here. Finding 40 is outstanding; 50 makes you a truly superb player; 55, and you are a paragon of gamesmanship!

(4 letters)

(5 letters)

(6 letters)

(7 letters)

6 "POPULARITY"

Find at least 100 words in this fun-fest. Come up with 75, and you're hot; nail 85, and you're totally rad; 90 or more, and you're a party animal!

(4 letters)   **(5 letters)**   **(6 letters)**

(7 letters)   **(8 letters)**

7 "HISTORICAL"

Hidden in this stumper are at least 112 words. Locate 70, and you're a scholar; score 80, and be a professor; discover 90, and you've got tenure!

(4 letters)

(5 letters)

(6 letters)

(7 letters)

(8 letters)

8 "CONCENTRATION"

At least 150 words can be found in the word above, including one 11-letter word! A total of 75 is good; 90 is excellent; and 110 means your powers of concentration are awesome!

(4 letters)   **(5 letters)**   **(6 letters)**

(7 letters)   **(8 letters)**

(9 letters)   **(10 letters)**   **(11 letters)**

9 "XYLOPHONE"

This noteworthy number will reveal at least 40 words. Find 25, and you've made the band; 30 hands you the baton; 35, you're Lionel Hampton!

(4 letters)   **(5 letters)**   **(6 letters)**

10 "NASTURTIUM"

As you tiptoe through the hothouse, look for at least 84 new words. Uncover 55, and you've got a green thumb; find 65, you're president of the garden club; cultivate 75, and you are a wordiculturist!

(4 letters)　　　　**(5 letters)**　　　　**(6 letters)**

(7 letters)　　　　**(8 letters)**

11 "WHISPERING"

You are likely to discover at least 84 words hiding here. Find 50, you're the sly one; uncover 60, and you're quite the detective; 70 proves you to be a master sleuth!

(4 letters)   **(5 letters)**   **(6 letters)**

(7 letters)   **(9 letters)**

12 "POLITICIAN"

The word above is concealing at least 86 words. A score of 40 is good; 50, excellent; and 60 means you win by a landslide!

(4 letters)   **(5 letters)**   **(6 letters)**

                                                                      (7 letters)

SOLITAIRE BATTLESHIPS: ENSIGN

13

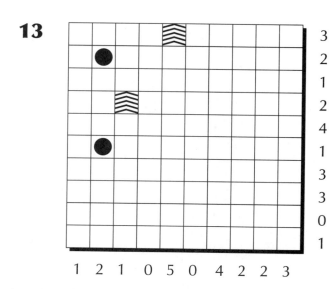

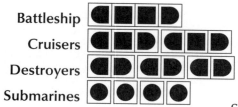

Battleship
Cruisers
Destroyers
Submarines

Solutions—Pages 213-216

14

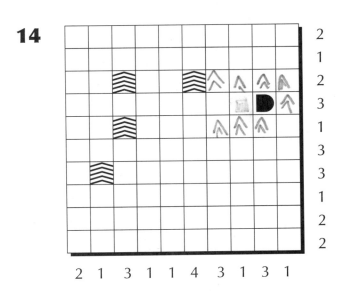

Grid 14 column clues (bottom): 2 1 3 1 1 4 3 1 3 1

Grid 14 row clues (right): 2 1 2 3 1 3 3 1 2 2

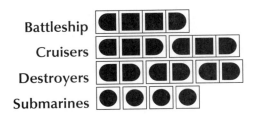

Battleship

Cruisers

Destroyers

Submarines

15

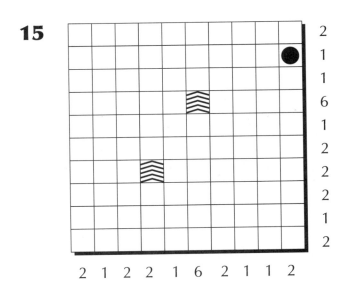

Grid 15 column clues (bottom): 2 1 2 2 1 6 2 1 1 2

Grid 15 row clues (right): 2 1 1 6 1 2 2 2 1 2

16

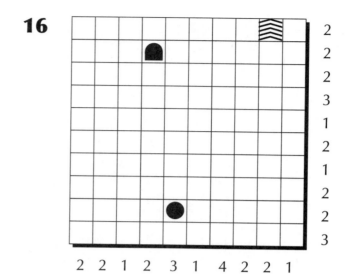

2
2
2
3
1
2
1
2
2
3

2 2 1 2 3 1 4 2 2 1

Battleship
Cruisers
Destroyers
Submarines

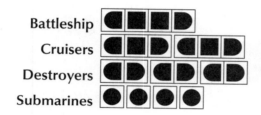

17

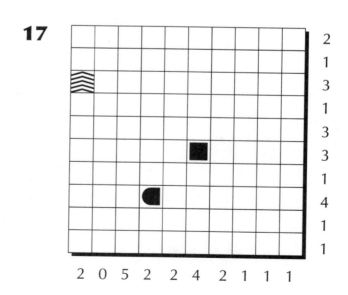

2
1
3
1
3
3
1
4
1
1

2 0 5 2 2 4 2 1 1 1

18

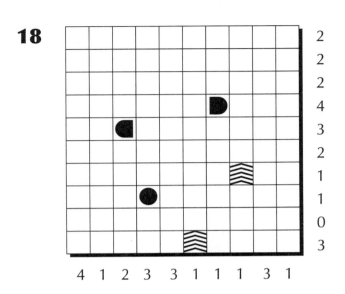

Battleship
Cruisers
Destroyers
Submarines

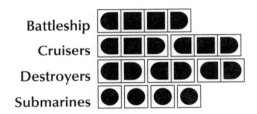

19

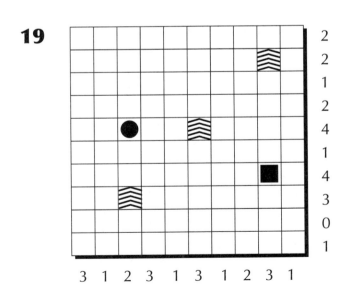

20

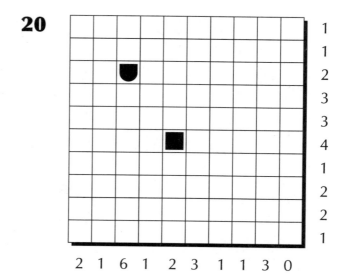

1
1
2
3
3
4
1
2
2
1

2 1 6 1 2 3 1 1 3 0

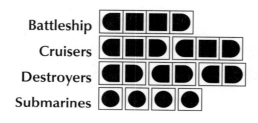

Battleship

Cruisers

Destroyers

Submarines

21

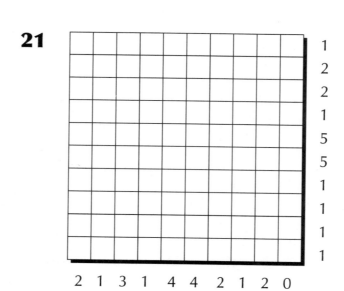

1
2
2
1
5
5
1
1
1
1

2 1 3 1 4 4 2 1 2 0

22

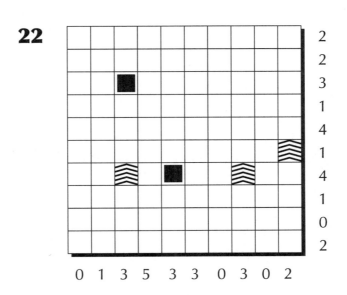

Columns: 0 1 3 5 3 3 0 3 0 2
Rows: 2 2 3 1 4 1 4 1 0 2

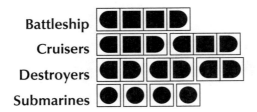

Battleship
Cruisers
Destroyers
Submarines

23

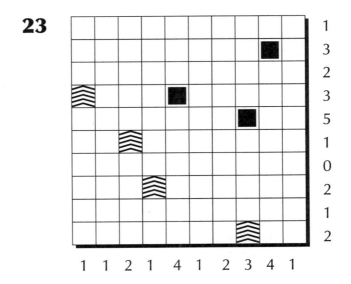

Columns: 1 1 2 1 4 1 2 3 4 1
Rows: 1 3 2 3 5 1 0 2 1 2

24

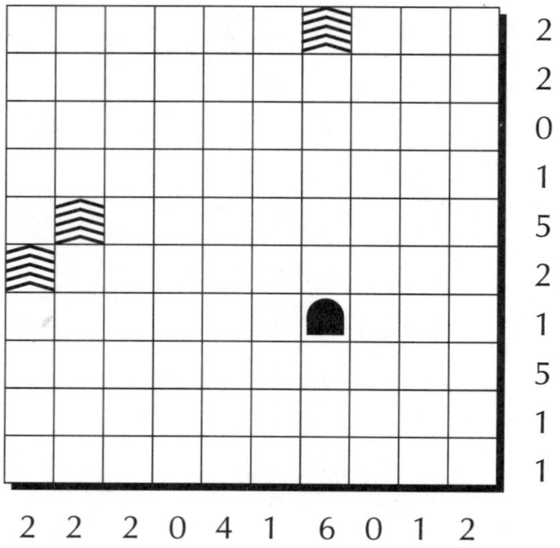
2
2
0
1
5
2
1
5
1
1
2 2 2 0 4 1 6 0 1 2

Battleship
Cruisers
Destroyers
Submarines

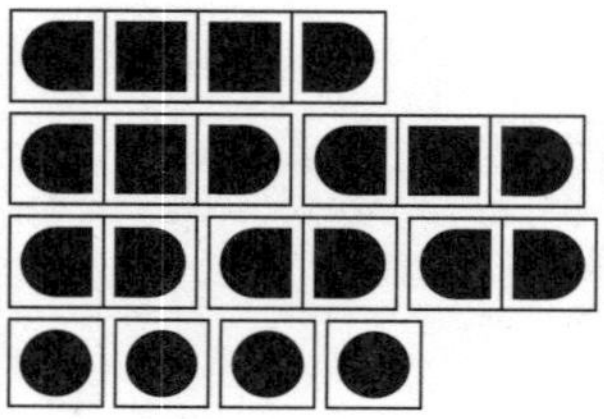

25

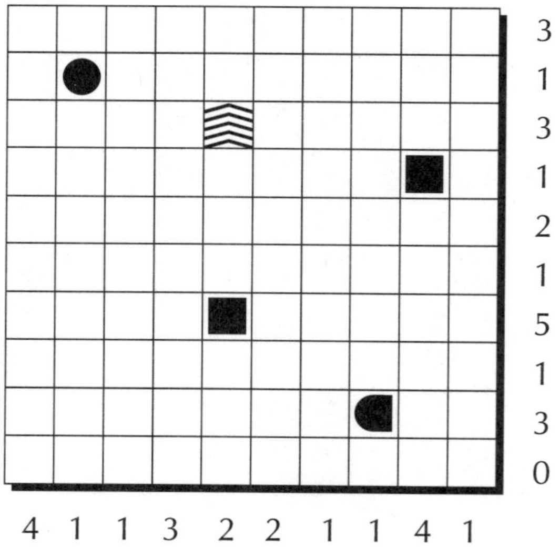
3
1
3
1
2
1
5
1
3
0
4 1 1 3 2 2 1 1 4 1

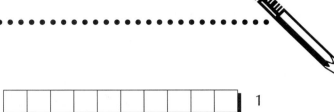

26

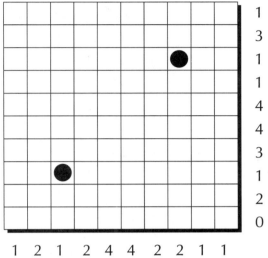

1
3
1
1
4
4
3
1
2
0

1 2 1 2 4 4 2 2 1 1

Battleship
Cruisers
Destroyers
Submarines

27

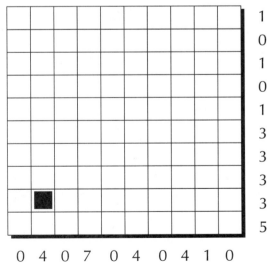

1
0
1
0
1
3
3
3
3
5

0 4 0 7 0 4 0 4 1 0

28

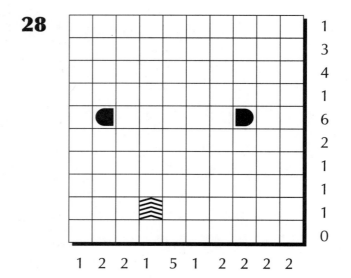

1
3
4
1
6
2
1
1
1
0

1 2 2 1 5 1 2 2 2 2

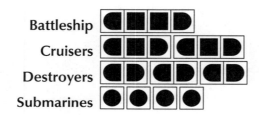

Battleship
Cruisers
Destroyers
Submarines

29

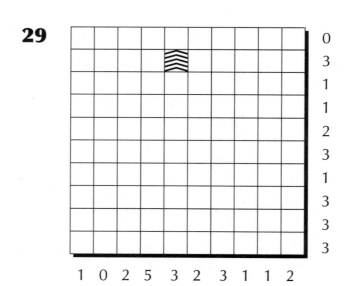

0
3
1
1
2
3
1
3
3
3

1 0 2 5 3 2 3 1 1 2

30

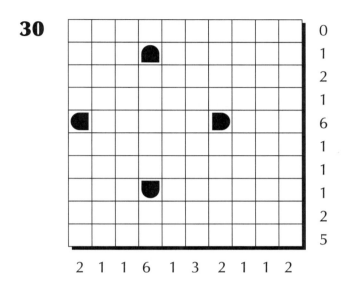

Right side (top to bottom): 0 1 2 1 6 1 1 1 2 5

Bottom (left to right): 2 1 1 6 1 3 2 1 1 2

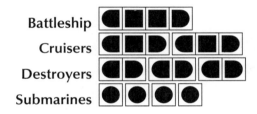

Battleship
Cruisers
Destroyers
Submarines

31

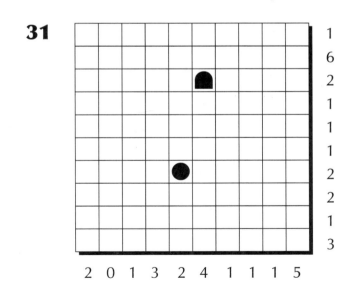

Right side (top to bottom): 1 6 2 1 1 1 2 2 1 3

Bottom (left to right): 2 0 1 3 2 4 1 1 1 5

123

32

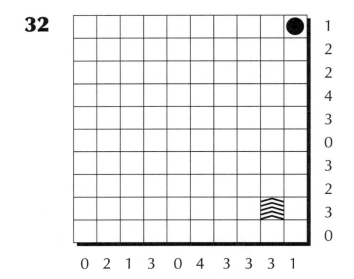

Grid 32 row clues (top to bottom): 1, 2, 2, 4, 3, 0, 3, 2, 3, 0

Grid 32 column clues (left to right): 0, 2, 1, 3, 0, 4, 3, 3, 3, 1

Battleship	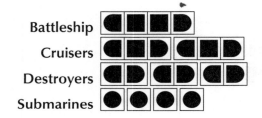
Cruisers	
Destroyers	
Submarines	

33

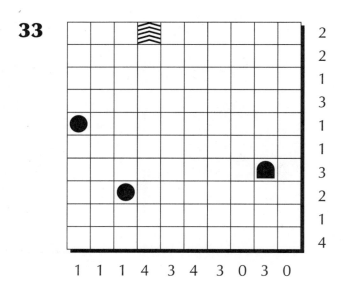

Grid 33 row clues (top to bottom): 2, 2, 1, 3, 1, 1, 3, 2, 1, 4

Grid 33 column clues (left to right): 1, 1, 1, 4, 3, 4, 3, 0, 3, 0

MORE MAZES

19

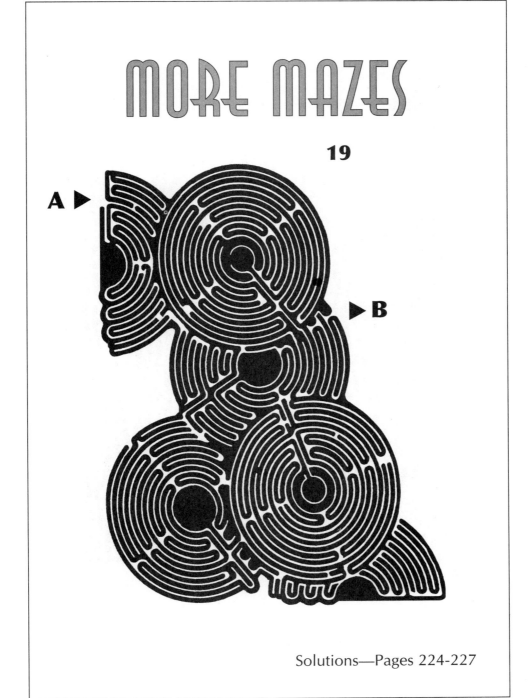

A ▶

▶ B

Solutions—Pages 224-227

20

21

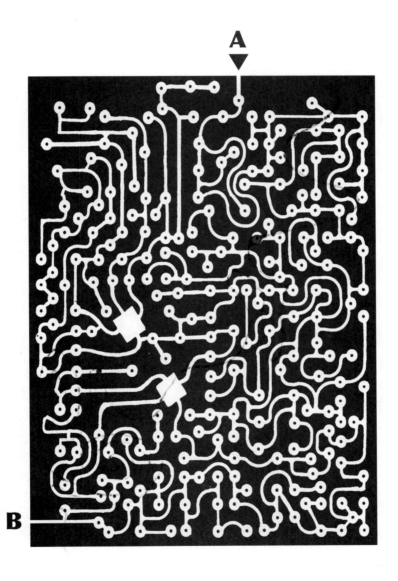

22

A

Find a route from A to B that passes every one of the stars. The route may pass each star once only.

B

23

A

B

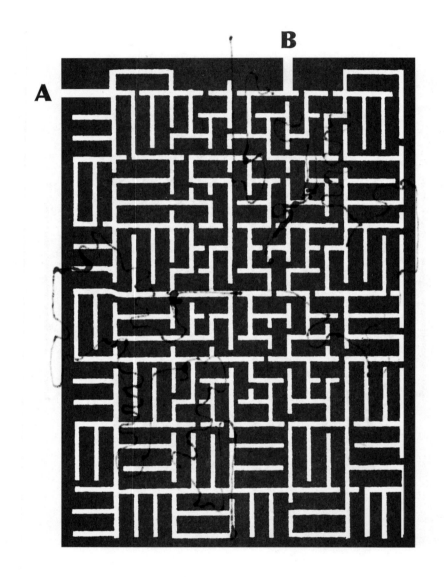

25

A

B

26

27

A

B

28

A

B

A

B

30

G

Begin at the bottom of the page
and find the other end of line G.

A   B   C D E F

WORD SEARCHES 2

"Guess the Theme"
GENERAL INSTRUCTIONS

To make things a bit trickier, the theme and the word list of three puzzles are a secret. It's up to you to figure out what the 20 items hidden in the grid are and what they have in common. To get you started, we'll tell you the first letter of each word or phrase and give you the appropriate number of blanks. For example, if the item were APPLE TREE, the hint would be A _ _ _ _ _ _ _ _.

After you loop an item in the grid, fill in the appropriate blanks below the grid to help you with the word list. If you find a word that doesn't fit in any of the blanks, ignore it: it's not part of the list. You may also find that more than one word will fit a particular set of blanks. If it doesn't have something in common with all the other entries, ignore it, too. To help you, the clue list, when completed, will be in alphabetical order. There is just one correct overall puzzle solution.

When you're done looping, read the unused letters from left to right, row by row, from top to bottom. They will spell out a message that reveals the theme.

Solutions—Pages 230-238

GUESS THE THEME 1

For instructions on how to solve Guess the Theme puzzles, see page 137. Hint: the grid itself resembles one of the hidden items. The word list is on page 230.

```
N T B H I B F L U T E
O L I F E S A V E R S
T S R     S E G A G E
E W D     I L E E O E
B S H S C H D B E L H
O S O I R E E H C F C
O E U S C L E E G G S
K R S R T U N O D R S
P C E I E D G     E I
A I O H K N N     E W
P A S S C T I H I N S
E N         O G W A R T S
R R       P S E W R T I
T H I H N O S E E T O
N O T T U B L N E S S
```

B A G E L   N _ _ _
B E L T   N _ _ _ _ _ _ _ _ _ _ _ _
B I R D H O U S E   P _ _ _ _ _ _ _ _ _
B U T T O N   P _ _ _ _ _
C _ _ _ _ _ _ _   S _ _ _ _ _ _ _ _ _ _
D _ _ _ _   S _ _ _
F _ _ _ _   S _ _ _ _ _ _ _
G _ _ _ _ _ _ _ _   S _ _ _ _
L _ _ _ _ _ _ _ _ _   S _ _ _ _ _ _ _ _ _ _
N _ _ _   T _ _ _

THE LEGEND OF ARTHUR

```
A E R E V E N I U G A
R T X I H U R A M V L
D O S C N E W E A A E
E O S A A B R L L U K
R C A M E L O T L T A
D E T O I N I I P H L
R O U N D T A B L E E
O U L L K R T L U R H
M K N I G H T A H R T
E S N Y W D O N R Q F
C G L D O U N C U T O
M O R G A N L E F A Y
H O U F T H S L G E D
R O M R A T S O T E A
O R U H T R A T N E L
```

ARMOR	LADY OF THE LAKE
ARTHUR	LANCELOT
AVALON	LEGEND
CAMELOT	MERLIN
COURT	MORDRED
EXCALIBUR	MORGAN LE FAY
GUINEVERE	QUEST
HOLY GRAIL	ROUND TABLE
KING	UTHER
KNIGHT	VISOR

FEELING LUCKY?

```
K N O C K O N W O O D
C F L L A B T H G I E
A I N D E M S I C S N
R T H I R T E E N U G
C A C A B K H E V P N
A A H D G S A U P E P
N C A E I N N E M R N
O Y N W B I S O R S T
P H C J I N X R O T U
E O E C G S A H T I S
T T G O U I H L B T R
S I N N R O B G I G
R A B B I T S F O O T
O O O D T B L E U N C
K W H O R S E S H O E
```

BIG BREAK	LOTTO
BINGO	OMEN
CHANCE	RABBIT'S FOOT
CHARM	RAINBOW
CURSE	SEVEN
DICE	STEP ON A CRACK
EIGHT BALL	STREAK
HORSESHOE	SUPERSTITION
JINX	THIRTEEN
KNOCK ON WOOD	WISHBONE

IT'S ELEMENTARY

```
W P H O S P H O R U S
H E O C A L T D O Y O
U R N T U R A N I U M
G I E T A I F T R Y O
Z O Y R T S I M E H C
U D S W A L S L B M N
S I L V E R M I M O E
W C A L C I U M U U G
R T E A I C I N N M O
I A U M O S D Y C O R
D B U P X G O E I T D
N L P A Y T S T M L Y
S E S A G E L B O N H
R O O M E I C G T P A
C H E N N O B R A C E
```

ATOMIC NUMBER
CALCIUM
CARBON
CHEMISTRY
COPPER
GOLD
HYDROGEN
ISOTOPE
LEAD
METALS

NEON
NOBLE GASES
OXYGEN
PERIODIC TABLE
PHOSPHORUS
POTASSIUM
SILVER
SODIUM
URANIUM
ZINC

GUESS THE THEME 2

For instructions on how to solve Guess the Theme puzzles, see page 137. Hint: the grid itself could be an item in the list. The word list is on page 230.

```
T  H  R  U  O  F  Y  B  O  W  T
C  L  N  E  L  G  R  E  I  D  A
O  E  N  A  P  W  O  D  N  I  W
M  W  G  M  N  A  D  S  O  A  L
I  O  A  T  L  T  G  H  H  O  D
C  T  V  P  A  E  R  E  L  U  R
S  H  T  I  H  M  E  E  M  E  A
T  C  E  E  E  S  E  T  N  T  C
R  A  R  C  H  S  I  C  E  S  T
I  E  A  E  R  N  C  E  A  D  S
P  B  L  R  O  U  S  R  O  L  O
U  F  A  P  L  L  Y  M  E  R  P
T  R  U  O  C  S  I  N  N  E  T
E  O  C  T  A  N  N  G  U  L  N
C  A  E  P  O  L  E  V  N  E  R
```

B _ _ _ _ _ _ _ _ _   P _ _ _
  B _ _ _ _ _ _ _   P _ _ _ _ _ _ _
C _ _ _ _ _ _ _ _ _   P _ _ _ _ _ _ _
  C _ _ _ _ _   R _ _ _ _ _ _
  D _ _ _ _ _   R _ _ _ _
  D _ _ _   S _ _ _ _
  E _ _ _ _ _ _ _   S _ _ _ _
  F _ _ _   T _ _ _ _ _ _ _ _ _ _
  M _ _ _   T _ _ - _ _ - _ _ _ _
M _ _ _ _ _ _ _ _ _ _   W _ _ _ _ _ _ _ _ _

DOG AND CAT SCAN

```
H E A T H C L I F F M
S W S H E N B E I U T
O L D Y E L L E R S R
C E A D L I L R N L Y
K P D P X V A P O J C
S I U M R Y E U I H I
E E N A G W E S E S N
B K O R T S A S T I G
A U Y T I T H I T E A
L D D S A I R N A Y R
I A N D R C I B P I F
N M S E Y T P O G C I
A R C S N T O O D I E
S A A I I N N T T D L
T M R D S E O S G S D
```

ASTRO	MURRAY
BENJI	ODIE
BUDDY	OLD YELLER
CHESHIRE CAT	PUSS IN BOOTS
EDDIE	RIN TIN TIN
FELIX	SNOOPY
GARFIELD	SOCKS
HEATHCLIFF	SYLVESTER
LASSIE	TOP CAT
MARMADUKE	TRAMP

STAR WARS

```
T T H E E M P I R E H
T E D A R K S I D E F
H I L L N M J E S T S
E Y P U A S A E R C T
F E P K B T O I D L O
O A L E H L L I I R
R S W S R O A G O W M
C S T K G D H A R O T
E A S Y P T R O D O R
R O O W S R L I F K O
O D N A L O L E V I O
A O B L F D S E B E P
B E N K E N O B I E E
R T A E R E W A R A R
S D A R T H V A D E R
```

BEN KENOBI
DARK SIDE
DARTH VADER
DEATH STAR
DROID
ENDOR
HAN SOLO
HYPERDRIVE
JEDI
LANDO

LEIA
LIGHTSABER
LUKE SKYWALKER
REBEL
STORMTROOPER
THE EMPIRE
THE FORCE
TRILOGY
WOOKIEE
YODA

"OH-OH!"

```
S O F O O T L O O S E
M E E O O T H O E R B
B A Z O O K A D O I O
U A B O L L E O G R W
K O Y R O D P F S A D
C O C O O N O R R K G
B E C U O O S C O O K
L O O P T H E L O O P
O O O O E T O D A B F
O T T O I S Y O O K O
P O S L A G O O N O O
E C D R O R L O O O O
R B O O B O O O M C G
S E D O O A N P O A D
D Y O M O V H D A D V
```

BAZOOKA
BIGFOOT
BLOOPERS
BOO-BOO
COCOON
COOKBOOK
DROOL
FOOLPROOF
FOOTLOOSE
GOODY-GOODY

IGLOO
KAZOO
LAGOON
LOOP-THE-LOOP
OOMPH
POOLROOM
SNOOZE
VAMOOSE
VOODOO
"YOO-HOO!"

BEACHY-KEEN

```
S  T  I  U  S  M  I  W  S  A  N
T  D  A  E  C  A  D  U  N  E  S
T  E  V  L  L  I  N  I  K  I  B
E  A  K  S  L  B  R  E  Q  D  U
W  B  I  N  L  E  R  N  R  U  B
O  E  O  O  A  T  R  A  H  S  R
T  E  C  D  B  L  U  B  E  E  T
R  K  H  I  Y  G  B  S  M  N  G
E  V  I  D  E  S  S  S  U  S
D  A  N  F  L  A  U  D  R  W  A
N  T  I  A  L  T  E  R  A  R  N
U  L  O  G  O  O  A  N  F  D  D
I  M  N  W  V  A  A  G  T  I  A
N  U  A  T  E  D  I  T  W  O  L
S  I  O  S  P  L  A  S  H  N  S
```

BIKINI	SANDALS
BLANKET	SPLASH
BODY SURF	SUNBLOCK
BURN	SUNGLASSES
DIVE	SWIMSUIT
DUNE	TOWEL
FLOAT	UMBRELLA
LIFEGUARD	UNDERTOW
LOW TIDE	VOLLEYBALL
RAFT	WAVES

GUESS THE THEME 3

For instructions on how to solve Guess the Theme puzzles, see page 137. The word list is on page 230.

```
T  H  T  N  A  E  G  R  E  S  W
E  D  G  R  B  R  I  E  D  T  A
E  I  I  S  I  F  B  I  I  L  R
L  L  E  A  L  E  R  E  G  I  T
O  D  W  I  L  T  S  H  Z  I  S
P  A  T  B  I  P  E  M  N  S  C
R  Q  M  B  A  R  C  O  D  E  A
E  U  T  H  R  A  C  C  O  O  N
B  A  T  A  D  A  T  B  A  E  D
R  F  L  I  B  W  A  A  Y  E  Y
A  R  K  L  A  W  S  S  O  R  C
B  E  S  F  L  F  K  S  O  E  A
R  S  O  F  L  U  R  T  E  F  N
N  H  H  A  N  A  V  A  E  E  E
S  T  R  K  I  P  G  E  P  R  S
```

A _ _ _ _ _ _ _ _   P _ _ _ _ _ _
        B _ _ _ _   P _ _ _ _
B _ _ _ _ _ _ _ _ _   R _ _ _ _ _ _
    B _ _ _ _ _ _   R _ _ _ _ _ _
            B _ _ _   S _ _ _ _ _ _ _
B _ _ _ _ _ _ _ _ _ _   S _ _ _ _
    B _ _ _ _ _ _ _   S _ _ _ _
C _ _ _ _ _ _ _ _   T _ _ _
    C _ _ _ _ _ _ _   T _ _ _ _
            F _ _ _   Z _ _ _ _

CASUAL DRESS

```
B T E W J S A R T E A
B A S E B A L L C A P
L L A H E N E A T E T
S N T R I B P R C I I
S O U S T R O H S K U
E V R S E T T S H S
R E T A E W S F A E P
D R L R T S F R T E M
N A E Q I O U T U S U
U L N I T K O O A R J
S L E U H L S M L E N
E S C A U W A I C B L
T E K C A J M I N E D
O I T H A S T H G I T
S L I P P E R S E S M
```

BASEBALL CAP
BELT
BLOUSE
CULOTTES
CUTOFFS
DENIM JACKET
JEANS
JUMPSUIT
KHAKIS
MINISKIRT

OVERALLS
PAJAMAS
SHORTS
SLACKS
SLIPPERS
SUNDRESS
SWEATER
TIGHTS
T-SHIRT
TURTLENECK

THE LOST WORLD

```
N O J T T X E R T F A
A S L U L C O D O I G
T U N O R T N S G G E
S R A L P A S I U R O
J U I A A I S S T S F
W A R C L A W S K X R
T S W E E R E E I H E
U O G S O R L E S C P
O L M E N E A W E R T
P L A N T E A T E R I
E A T O O H F E O L L
S I N Z L B E E L P E
S T E G O S A U R U S
O F A N G C K H I N C
K E E N Y S E L A C S
```

AGE OF REPTILES	PALEONTOLOGY
ALLOSAURUS	PLANT EATER
BONE	RAPTOR
CLAWS	SCALES
EGGS	SKELETON
EXTINCT	SKULL
FERNS	STEGOSAURUS
FOSSIL	TAIL
JAWS	T. REX
JURASSIC	TRICERATOPS

WRITE ON!

```
S  C  R  E  E  N  P  L  A  Y  D
U  R  T  L  I  N  N  G  A  S  T
S  O  R  C  E  I  O  O  K  H  O
N  C  T  I  E  T  I  I  V  C  D
I  O  I  T  S  A  T  I  R  E  O
B  M  T  R  I  S  P  E  R  E  L
I  P  I  A  Y  G  I  H  R  P  I
O  O  M  E  M  L  R  T  M  S  S
G  S  T  N  O  W  C  E  N  R  T
R  I  I  I  T  R  S  E  M  T  O
A  T  O  Z  R  S  E  V  U  I  S
P  I  L  A  A  S  R  P  L  T  L
H  O  E  G  S  A  P  N  O  D  W
Y  N  E  A  I  L  B  R  C  R  U
R  W  Y  M  R  I  Y  G  H  T  T
```

BIOGRAPHY	NOVEL
COLUMN	POEM
COMPOSITION	PRESCRIPTION
ESSAY	REPORT
LETTER	SATIRE
LYRICS	SCREENPLAY
MAGAZINE ARTICLE	SKIT
MEMO	SPEECH
MESSAGE	STORY
NOTE	TO-DO LIST

SCHOOL SUPPLIES

```
S  U  S  P  P  K  L  Y  L  C  H
P  A  P  E  R  C  L  I  P  I  C
R  D  I  R  S  O  C  A  G  S  N
O  T  R  P  E  N  S  H  H  S  U
T  C  A  A  E  T  L  A  N  C  P
R  M  L  P  O  I  N  R  A  R  E
A  D  N  D  G  B  E  I  E  U  L
C  P  O  H  F  D  K  K  O  A  O
T  D  T  S  N  S  R  C  T  P  H
O  E  E  I  E  A  U  A  A  S  I
R  N  B  S  M  L  G  P  A  L  C
E  A  O  L  K  C  A  K  U  L  B
L  R  O  T  A  L  U  C  L  A  C
U  A  K  T  O  E  R  A  S  E  R
R  T  E  S  T  T  U  B  E  S  R
```

BACKPACK	MARKER
BINDER	PAPER CLIP
BLACKBOARD	PENCIL
CALCULATOR	PENS
CHALK	POINTER
DESK	PROTRACTOR
ERASER	RULER
HIGHLIGHTER	SCALES
HOLE PUNCH	SPIRAL NOTEBOOK
MAPS	TEST TUBES

BY THE NUMBERS

```
E C A R D E G G E L 3
T H 2 E E E 3 2 S P 2
3 D 5 O T 9 I T E O 1
2 W O H G F 4 A B E S
S S A S B C T S A A A
E L L Y E D E 9 B 1 Y
S 1 S M B V 4 E Y E S
S E T E I U C O L B A
A U Y L 1 A L W O A E
L Y 9 K T T I B N C C
G 4 H C L U B K 5 O E
D T H U 2 S O 1 L N A
3 2 1 B L A S T O F F
2 B Y 2 O E 4 I N N G
7 4 4 1 7 5 E K A T 1
```

BABYLON 5
CATCH-22
COLT .45
EASY AS 1, 2, 3
49ER
4-EYES
4-H CLUB
9 LIVES
9 TO 5
1-ON-1

1, 2, BUCKLE MY SHOE
R2-D2
TAKE 5
3-D GLASSES
3-LEGGED RACE
3-PEAT
3-2-1 BLASTOFF!
3-WAY BULB
2-BY-4
2 IF BY SEA

GREAT BEGINNINGS

GENERAL INSTRUCTIONS

With these games, use the definitions to help you identify the words that begin with the specified letters.

Solutions—Pages 244-245

1 "IN"

Using the definitions listed below, identify these words that begin with IN.

1. Stimulus; motive   IN_____
2. True identity concealed or disguised   IN_____
3. Reliable; never wrong   IN_____
4. Establishment providing food and lodging   IN_____
5. Itemized list of goods   IN_____
6. Unafraid; bold; fearless   IN_____
7. Person who meddles in others' affairs   IN_____
8. Abnormal inability to sleep   IN_____
9. To receive as an heir   IN_____
10. Person confined to an institution or asylum   IN_____
11. Feebleness; weakness   IN_____
12. Measure of length; equal to $\frac{1}{12}$ foot   IN_____
13. To hurt or inflict physical harm   IN_____
14. Inactive; without power to move   IN_____
15. To examine by formal questioning   IN_____
16. Very young child; baby   IN_____
17. To sit on and hatch, as in eggs   IN_____
18. Raging fire; hellish   IN_____
19. Deep violet-blue   IN_____
20. The Hoosier state   IN_____
21. Group of foot soldiers   IN_____
22. Legally charge with a crime   IN_____
23. Colored liquid used for writing   IN_____

2 "EX"

Using the definitions listed below, identify these words that begin with EX.

1. To dismiss; to _____ from school — EX*PEL*
2. The way out — EX*IT*
3. Free from obligation; excused — EX*CEPTION*
4. "Bill and Ted's _____ Adventure" — EX*CITING*
5. Overstate; make something better than it is — EX*aggerate*
6. More or better than normal — EX*TRA-ORDINARY*
7. Test or quiz — EX*AM*
8. Process to discover something unknown — EX*PLORE*
9. Facial movement that reveals thoughts — EX*PRESSION*
10. Minimize; apologize — EX*cuse*
11. Second book of the Old Testament — EX*ODUS*
12. Costly; high priced — EX*PENSIVE*
13. Prolonged banishment — EX*ILE*
14. Precise; accurate — EX*act*
15. King Arthur's sword — EX*CALIBUR*
16. E.T. is one; alien being — EX*TRA TERESTRIAL*
17. Enlarge; grow — EX*PAND*
18. Great fatigue or weariness — EX*HAUSTED*
19. Highway for high-speed traffic — EX*PRESS WAY*
20. One who carries out death penalty — EX*ECUTIONER*
21. To send goods from one country to another — EX*PORT*
22. Not an introvert — EX*TROVERT*

3 "QU"

Using the definitions listed below, identify these words that begin with QU.

1.	Wet, boggy ground	QU_____
2.	A group of four	QU_____
3.	Bedcover stitched in patterns	QU_____
4.	Sound a duck makes	QU_____
5.	Shake; tremble	QU_____
6.	Not noisy; hushed	QU_____
7.	Angry dispute	QU_____
8.	Wet, deep sand deposit	QU_____
9.	Most powerful chess piece	QU_____
10.	State of uncertainty; dilemma	QU_____
11.	Society of Friends member	QU_____
12.	Imposed isolation	QU_____
13.	Small game bird	QU_____
14.	Stone or slate is excavated from this	QU_____
15.	Nazi collaborator; traitor	QU_____
16.	Drink deeply and heartily	QU_____
17.	Peculiarity	QU_____
18.	Question; inquiry	QU_____
19.	Line up	QU_____
20.	Pleasingly odd and old-fashioned	QU_____
21.	Subdue; allay	QU_____
22.	Malaria treatment	QU_____
23.	Yellowish apple-shaped fruit	QU_____
24.	Football team leader	QU_____
25.	Witty remark	QU_____

4 "WA"

Using the definitions listed below, identify these words that begin with WA.

1. Erratic, eccentric, irrational (slang)   WA_____

2. Thin, crisp cracker   WA_____

3. Apple, celery, and walnut mixture   WA_____

4. Carry or propel lightly   WA_____

5. Female who serves restaurant patrons   WA_____

6. Four-wheeled vehicle   WA_____

7. Child without home or friends   WA_____

8. Massive sea animal of the seal family   WA_____

9. Small kangaroo   WA_____

10. Roundish nut with two-lobed shell   WA_____

11. Unchaste; lewd   WA_____

12. Person looking on at a dance   WA_____

13. Yellow substance secreted by bees   WA_____

14. Fleshy flap of skin hanging from throat   WA_____

15. Person's supply of clothes   WA_____

16. Frame with ridged metal used for cleaning   WA_____

17. Sing like a bird   WA_____

18. Path taken by North American Indians on warlike expedition   WA_____

19. First U.S. president   WA_____

20. Sorcerer; wizard   WA_____

21. Longing or urge to travel   WA_____

22. Ballroom dance   WA_____

5 "SH"

Using the definitions listed below, identify these words that begin with SH.

1. Darkness cast upon a surface — SH adow
2. Frozen watered fruit juice and sugar — SH
3. English dramatist and poet; bard of Avon — SHakespeare
4. Onionlike plant used for flavoring — SH allops
5. Person who uses unethical or tricky methods — SH
6. Fragment; broken piece — SH ARD
7. Cloth used to wrap corpse for burial — SHrowd
8. Neglect; evade an obligation — SH IRK
9. Shell fragments scattered by explosion — SH ards
10. Fraud; imitation or counterfeit — SH
11. Tomb of saint or revered person — SHrine
12. British silver coin — SHILLING
13. Gesture indicating indifference — SHRUG
14. County's chief law enforcement officer — SHERRIEF
15. Plant; bush — SHRUB
16. Bunch of cut stalks of grain — SH
17. Young pig — SH
18. Used in baked goods — SHORTENING
19. Sharp, piercing cry or scream — SHRIEK
20. Small, long-tailed crustacean — SHRIMP
21. Nagging, evil-tempered woman — SH
22. Scrupulously avoid — SH

6 "PO"

Using the definitions listed below, identify these words that begin with PO.

1.   Written expression, usually rhyming — PO em
2.   White, translucent, hard earthenware — PO TTERY
3.   Spirit; ghost — PO ltergeist
4.   Device measuring pulse; lie detector — PO
5.   To cook unbroken egg in water — PO ach
6.   Hawaiian food made of mashed taro root — PO
7.   Pope or high priest — PO
8.   Flat portable case used for carrying — PO
9.   Yellow powderlike cells on flower stamens — PO llen
10. Animal covered with sharp spines — PO rcupine
11. Painting of person, usually the face — PO rtrait
12. Position of body parts — PO se
13. Popular card game — PO ker
14. Nonsense (slang) — PO sh
15. Hairdo; hair swept high off forehead — PO
16. Fast dance using specific music — PO lka
17. Body of men who assist sheriff — PO lice
18. The North Star — PO LARIS
19. Leading Communist Party committee — PO
20. Former mail delivery system using horses — PO ny express

159

7 "MA"

Using the definitions listed below, identify these words that begin with MA.

1. Authoritative order or command — MA_____
2. Small South American monkey — MA_____
3. Short love poem that can be set to music — MA_____
4. Hard metamorphic limestone — MA_____
5. Hypothetical inhabitant of Mars — MA_____
6. Man in charge of royal household — MA_____
7. One who chooses suffering rather than compromising principles — MA_____
8. Young Caroline Kennedy's pony — MA_____
9. Fat Tuesday; carnival day in New Orleans — MA_____
10. Manage or plan skillfully; scheme — MA_____
11. Intricate network of pathways — MA_____
12. Disease caused by infectious mosquito bite — MA_____
13. Tract of low, wet soft land — MA_____
14. Tragedy by Shakespeare — MA_____
15. Long distance or endurance contest — MA_____
16. Care of fingernails — MA_____
17. Rhythmic ballroom dance — MA_____
18. Cocktail made of gin and dry vermouth — MA_____
19. Purple and red mixture — MA_____

8 "FO"

Using the definitions listed below, identify these words that begin with FO.

1. Young horse   FO_____
2. Lack of sense or rational conduct   FO_____
3. One's strong point   FO_____
4. Creamy sauce used for dipping   FO_____
5. Imitate for purposes of fraud   FO_____
6. Field team game played with pigskin   FO_____
7. Enemy; opponent   FO_____
8. Comment or reference at bottom of page   FO_____
9. For eternity; always; endlessly   FO_____
10. Bowl holding water in baptismal
    services   FO_____
11. Leaves, as of a plant or tree   FO_____
12. Tract of land covered by trees   FO_____
13. Small tongs or pincers for grasping,
    pulling   FO_____
14. Weakness in character; frailty   FO_____
15. Coarse food for cattle, horses   FO_____
16. Chain attached to watch   FO_____
17. To search for food or provisions   FO_____
18. Child found after parental abandonment   FO_____
19. Two weeks   FO_____
20. Hardened remains of ancient life   FO_____
21. Plant with small blue flowers   FO_____
22. Prohibit; rule against   FO_____

9 "NO"

Using the definitions listed below, identify these words that begin with NO.

1.	Flat, narrow strip of dough	NO_____
2.	Longing for something long ago	NO_____
3.	Eleventh month of calendar year	NO_____
4.	Cut in edge or surface	NO_____
5.	In the Bible, patriarch commanded to build an Ark	NO_____
6.	Party's candidate in election	NO_____
7.	Harmful to health	NO_____
8.	Casually indifferent; without concern	NO_____
9.	Clamor; din	NO_____
10.	Special prayers and devotions	NO_____
11.	Christmas expression of joy	NO_____
12.	Swedish inventor of dynamite	NO_____
13.	Loop formed in rope	NO_____
14.	Small spout of hose	NO_____
15.	Pen name; pseudonym	NO_____
16.	Official authorized to attest documents	NO_____
17.	Sugar and nut confection	NO_____
18.	Brief written statement to aid memory	NO_____
19.	Wanderer	NO_____
20.	Functioning at night	NO_____
21.	Person new to activity; apprentice	NO_____
22.	Northern end of earth's axis	NO_____
23.	Small knot or rounded lump	NO_____

SAY IT AGAIN, SAM

GENERAL INSTRUCTIONS

In each of the following grids, five synonyms or words similar in meaning can be found. Following the example and using the clue letters provided in each puzzle, complete the words.

Solutions—Page 246

EXAMPLE:

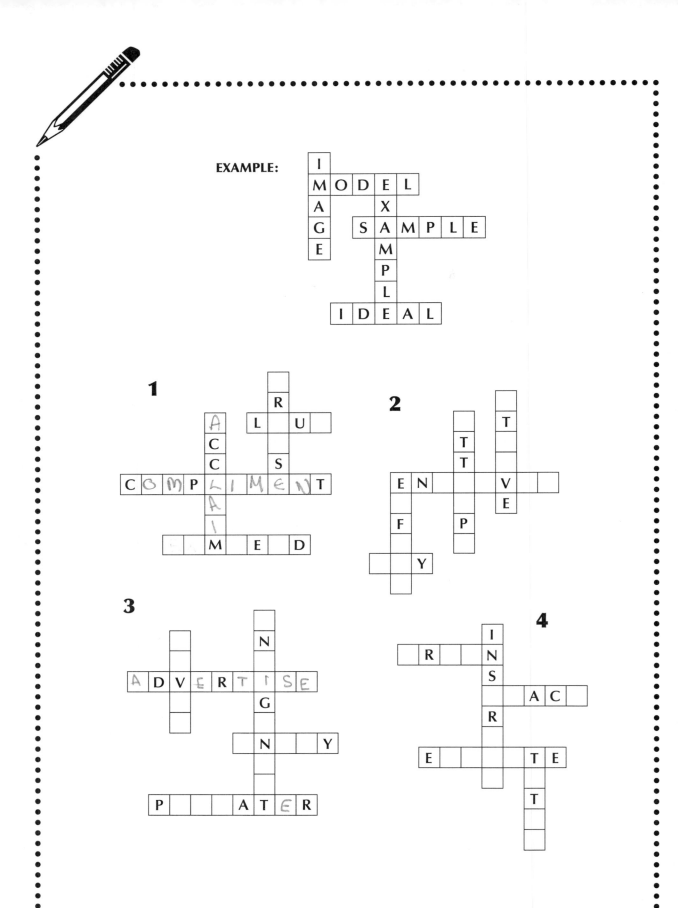

1

2

3

4

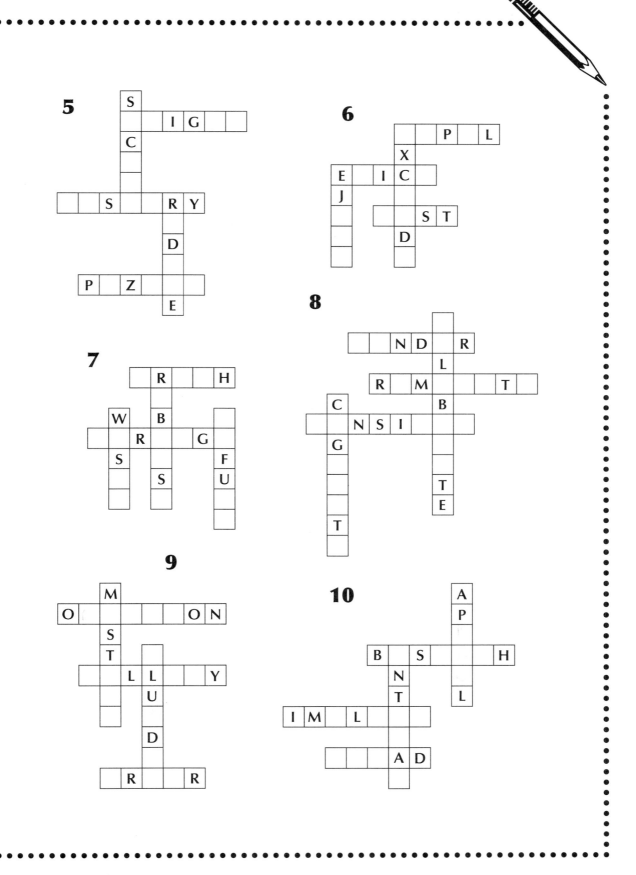

5

6

7

8

9

10

165

SOLITAIRE BATTLESHIPS: COMMODORE

34

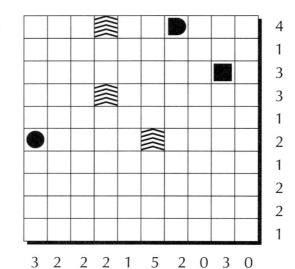

Grid column totals: 3 2 2 2 1 5 2 0 3 0

Grid row totals: 4 1 3 3 1 2 1 2 2 1

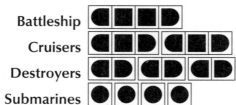

Battleship
Cruisers
Destroyers
Submarines

Solutions—Pages 216-219

35

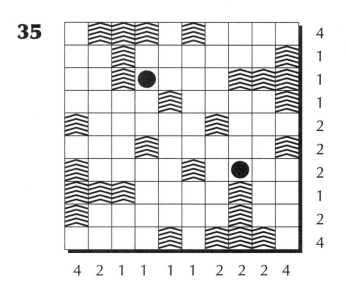

4
1
1
1
2
2
2
1
2
4

4 2 1 1 1 1 2 2 2 4

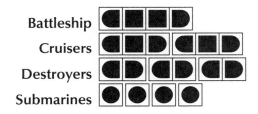

Battleship

Cruisers

Destroyers

Submarines

36

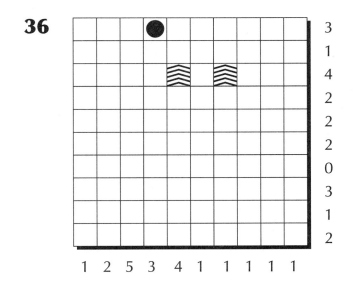

3
1
4
2
2
2
0
3
1
2

1 2 5 3 4 1 1 1 1 1

37

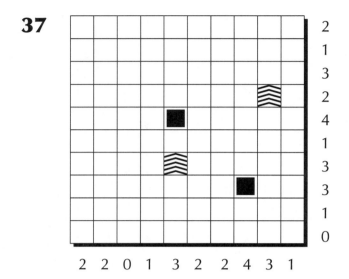

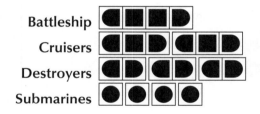

Battleship

Cruisers

Destroyers

Submarines

38

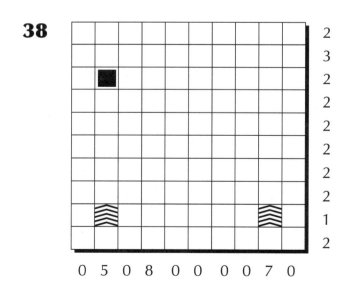

39

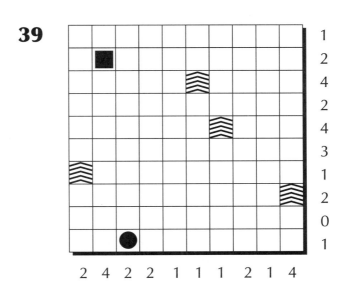

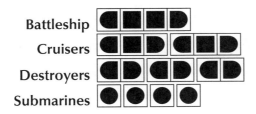

Battleship
Cruisers
Destroyers
Submarines

40

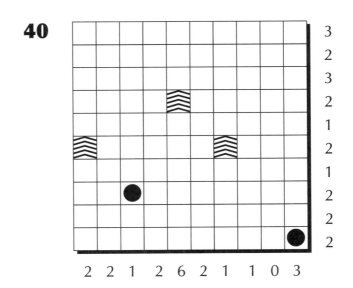

41

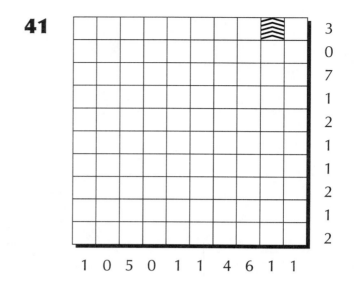

3 0 7 1 2 1 1 2 1 2

1 0 5 0 1 1 4 6 1 1

Battleship
Cruisers
Destroyers
Submarines

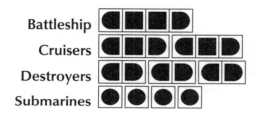

42

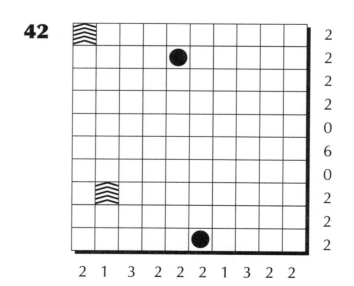

2 2 2 2 0 6 0 2 2 2

2 1 3 2 2 2 1 3 2 2

43

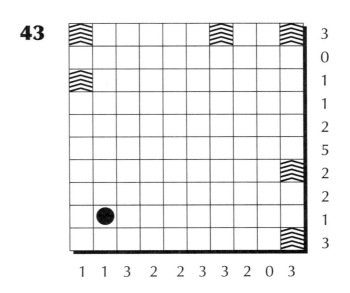

Row clues (top to bottom): 3, 0, 1, 1, 2, 5, 2, 2, 1, 3

Column clues (left to right): 1, 1, 3, 2, 2, 3, 3, 2, 0, 3

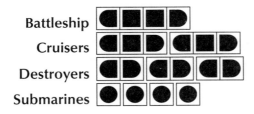

Battleship
Cruisers
Destroyers
Submarines

44

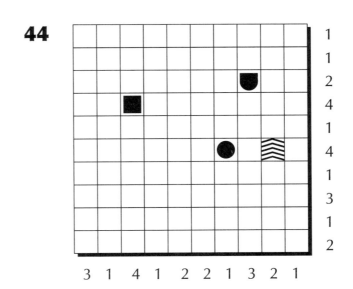

Row clues (top to bottom): 1, 1, 2, 4, 1, 4, 1, 3, 1, 2

Column clues (left to right): 3, 1, 4, 1, 2, 2, 1, 3, 2, 1

45

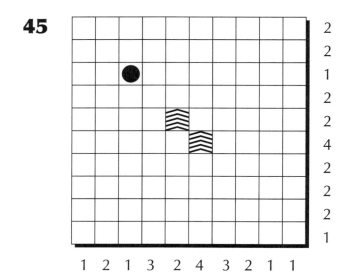

Right column (top to bottom): 2 2 1 2 2 4 2 2 2 1

Bottom row (left to right): 1 2 1 3 2 4 3 2 1 1

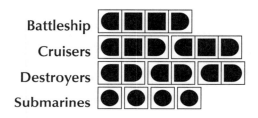

Battleship	
Cruisers	
Destroyers	
Submarines	

46

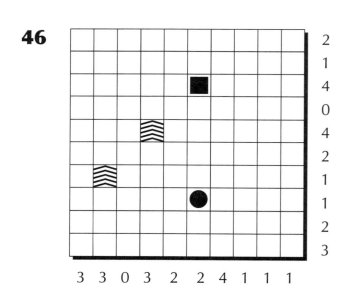

Right column (top to bottom): 2 1 4 0 4 2 1 1 2 3

Bottom row (left to right): 3 3 0 3 2 2 4 1 1 1

47

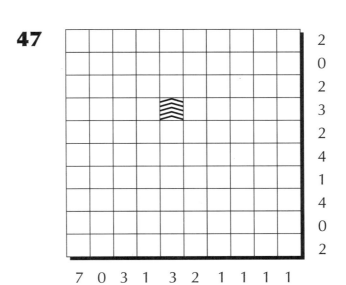

2 0 2 3 2 4 1 4 0 2

7 0 3 1 3 2 1 1 1 1

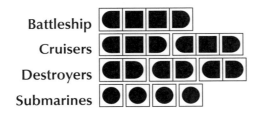

Battleship
Cruisers
Destroyers
Submarines

48

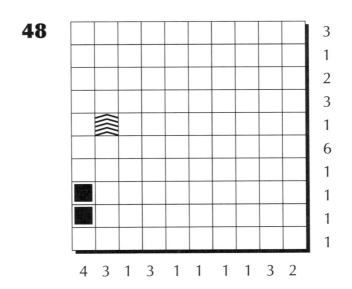

3 1 2 3 1 6 1 1 1 1

4 3 1 3 1 1 1 1 3 2

49

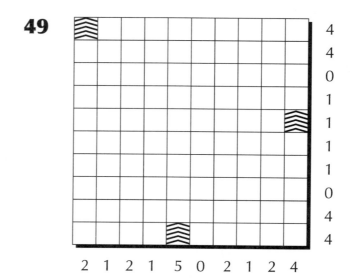

										4
										4
										0
										1
										1
										1
										1
										0
										4
										4

2 1 2 1 5 0 2 1 2 4

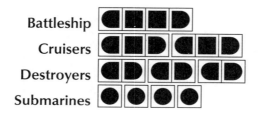

Battleship
Cruisers
Destroyers
Submarines

50

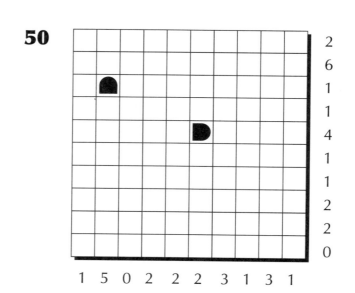

1 5 0 2 2 2 3 1 3 1

174

51

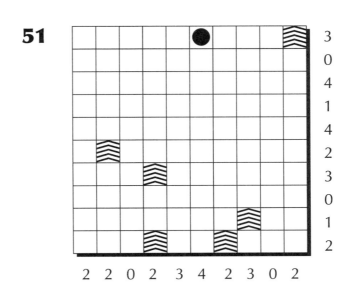

3
0
4
1
4
2
3
0
1
2

2 2 0 2 3 4 2 3 0 2

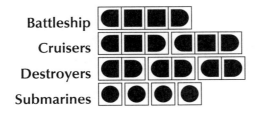

Battleship

Cruisers

Destroyers

Submarines

52

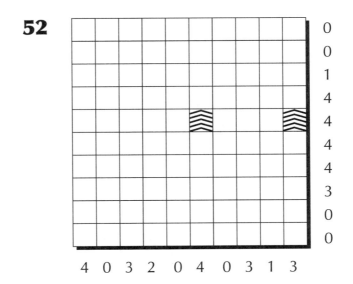

0
0
1
4
4
4
4
3
0
0

4 0 3 2 0 4 0 3 1 3

53

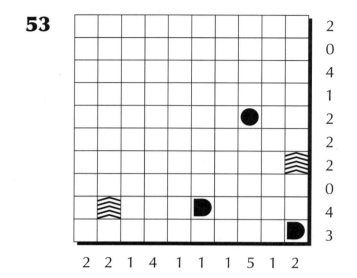

Right column (top to bottom): 2 0 4 1 2 2 2 0 4 3

Bottom row (left to right): 2 2 1 4 1 1 1 5 1 2

Battleship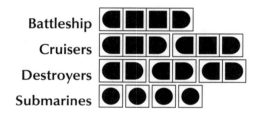
Cruisers
Destroyers
Submarines

54

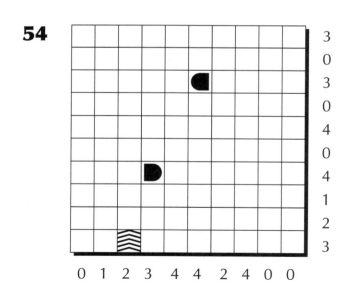

Right column (top to bottom): 3 0 3 0 4 0 4 1 2 3

Bottom row (left to right): 0 1 2 3 4 4 2 4 0 0

CLEVER WHODUNITS

Solutions—Page 229

THE REAL McCOY

The men were in the den sipping coffee or root beer. Dr. J. L. Quicksolve had invited several friends for dinner. Since Benjamin Clayborn Blowhard was making his nest on Sergeant Rebekah Shurshot's couch for the week, he was also invited. As usual, Blowhard was doing the talking—this time about his ancestors.

"The men on my father's side were nomadic adventurers like I am," he said. He had spoken of that side of his family before. According to him, his family spread across the globe, meeting and aiding, instructing, or encouraging more famous people than are found in a series of John Jakes novels.

"My mother's side was a little more stable," he went on, "living and prospering in the beautiful state of Virginia. Their name was McCoy. In fact, the expression 'the real McCoy' came from the honesty and integrity of my great-grandfather McCoy, who was once nominated for governor."

Dr. Quicksolve almost choked on his coffee. He sat next to Junior, who smiled and winked knowingly. Captain Reelumin, Lieutenant Rootumont, and Fred Fraudstop listened attentively. Fred was hoping for the chance to talk about his ancestors. His chances were slim. Blowhard seemed to have an endless supply of air and continued talking without the usual necessity of taking a breath.

"Why don't you tell him, Dad?" Junior whispered to Dr. Quicksolve.

What does Junior think Dr. Quicksolve should say?

BEN AGAIN

It was Benjamin Clayborn Blowhard's last night in town. He would be off to "the East" in the morning. For "government reasons" he could not say exactly where he was going. Also "for government reasons" he could not say what he did for the government.

Sergeant Rebekah Shurshot had invited Blowhard and Dr. Quicksolve out to dinner. Dr. Quicksolve reluctantly accepted, to avoid hurting her feelings. As they listened to the end of another of Blowhard's stories, Rebekah said, "You certainly are a man of adventure."

"I come by it honestly," Blowhard replied. Dr. Quicksolve cringed at the thought of hearing more about Blowhard's forefathers. "My ancestors were rugged individuals. My great-great-grandfather was a sheriff back in the late 1800s. One story my father

179

used to tell about him was when he was almost killed standing over his mother's grave. He was alone at the small cemetery. He took off his hat and held it reverently over his heart. That is what saved him. A bullet, fired by a vengeful desperado my great-great-grandfather had arrested for murder years before, slammed into his wristwatch. His wrist was bruised badly, but the watch saved his life.

"He drew his Colt 45s and shot the gun out of the bad guy's hand. They both mounted their horses, and the chase began. Great-great-grandfather caught up with the killer and dove out of his saddle, bringing the man down off his horse and to the ground. The fistfight lasted 20 minutes before that outlaw gave up because he just could not swing his arms any more. Both his eyes were so swollen from receiving punches that he could not see what he was swinging at!"

Dr. Quicksolve excused himself from the table to avoid laughing out loud.

What was wrong with Ben Blowhard's story this time?

in this 1800s there were no wristwatches

180

JOKERS WILD

The snowing had just begun, but the bitter winter wind forced Dr. J. L. Quicksolve to grab his hat with one hand and hold his collar closed with the other as he got out of his VW Beetle and walked past the ice-frosted car in the driveway. He walked carefully up the icy steps to the door of the house.

Miss Forkton opened the door when he rang the bell. He introduced himself, and she invited him in. "It sure is cold out there," he said.

"Too cold for burglars, you would think," came her reply.

"Tell me about your robbery, Miss Forkton," Dr. Quicksolve said as he took off his coat. Miss Forkton took his coat and laid it on top of her own fur coat on a chair next to the phone table.

"Well, I just got home a few minutes ago. When I came in the door and saw my safe open," she said, pointing to an open wall safe, "I went straight to the phone and called you. I am glad you could get here so fast."

"Yes, we may have a hot trail for such a cold night," Quicksolve mused.

"I had a fortune in jewels stolen, Dr. Quicksolve. I don't think this is a good time for jokes!" she said.

"I agree with you one hundred percent. So why did you bring me out on such a cold night for this joke of yours, Miss Forkton?" the detective asked.

Why did he mistrust Miss Forkton?

THREAT

It was not the first time Dr. J. L. Quicksolve had received a threatening leter. This one, though, seemed a litle more menacing than the usual prank. It contained a small piece of plastic that was a bit of casing from a cylinder of dynamite.

Dr. Quicksolve had taken steps to protect himself. He left his VW Beetle parked on the street as a temptation for the would-be bomber. He set up a video camera in his upstairs window to watch his car through the night and keep a taped record.

Others were watching too. Sergeant Rebekah Shurshot drove the unmarked police car through the dark neighborhood. Officer Longarm sat beside her. They were going to drive by Dr. Quicksolve's house "just to see if anything looked suspicious." They knew about the threat and were worried about their friend.

As they drove closer to the house, thet saw a large sedan about half a block behind Dr. Quicksolve's VW. The car was dark. They did not realize it was occupied by two men until they were beside it. The small flame of a lighter flickered up to a cigarette on the passenger's side.

"Let's check this out," Sergeant Shurshot said, pulling up in front of the parked car.

She approached the driver's door. Officer Longarm went around to the other side. The driver's window came down. The smiling, mustached driver spoke. "Hi. We're lost, and we stopped to look at our map," he said, holding a map up to prove his point. "Could you help us out?"

Sergeant Shurshot was not smiling when she said, "Please get out of the car slowly with your hands up."

The two men looked at the officers and their drawn guns and did what they were told.

What tipped off the officers?

PLUNGER AND SNAKE

Dr. J. L. Quicksolve got out of his car. He pulled his hat down tighter on his head to avoid losing it to the icy wind on another snowy winter morning. He walked between the two police cars to the front door of Plunger and Snake's Plumbing Supplies. He pulled the front door open and walked in.

Lieutenant Rootumout was talking with a man who played with his mustache nervously as he spoke. Another officer was kneeling over a body on the floor. Lieutenant Rootumout looked up at Dr. Quicksolve and introduced him to Paul Plunger, the mustached man. Indicating the body, Lieutenant Rootumout said, "Stan Snake."

Dr. Quicksolve sat down and listened to Plunger's story. Plunger paused and rolled up his shirt sleeves. "Yes," he said, "I saw Stan's body when I came in this morning, but I did not have time to do anything. Someone had been hiding behind the door and stuck a gun in my back. He made me lie facedown on the floor. Then he left."

"Did he take anything?" Lieutenant Rootumout asked.

"I don't know. We don't keep any money here overnight, if that is what you mean. Maybe that is why he killed Stan—because he could not give him any money. The killer would not know our secretary, Miss Supplewrist, takes the day's earnings to the bank after we close. She brings money for petty cash when she comes to work every morning. She has not come in yet today," Mr. Plunger explained, giving his mustache a final tug.

"We'll talk to her when she arrives," Lieutenant Rootumout said.

"We'll ask if she has any idea why you killed your partner," Dr. Quicksolve added.

Why did Dr. Quicksolve suspect Plunger killed Snake?

SHORTSTOP'S BIKE

Junior got off his bike and knocked on his friend Shortstop's front door. Shortstop was usually sitting on his bike in the driveway when Junior came by, and they would ride to school together each morning. "Where's your bike?" Junior asked when Shortstop came to the door with his backpack in his hand and a sad look on his face.

"Somebody stole it from our garage yesterday afternoon," Shortstop said.

"Did you see anything?" Junior asked.

"No," Shortstop answered, "but my sister did. She heard a noise and looked out the window just in time to see a kid riding off on my bike. She doesn't know who it was, though. She only saw his back. She said he had on a denim jacket. It could have been anyone."

"We can check the bikes at school," Junior said as he pushed his bike down the sidewalk beside Shortstop.

Prissy Powers, the cutest girl on the cheerleading squad, was standing by the long row of bikes behind the school. "Hi, Junior. Hi, Shortstop. How come you're walking?"

"My bike was stolen yesterday," Shortstop said.

"I think we'll find it," Junior said confidently as he walked down the long row of bikes, stroking the crossbar of the first one of many that looked like Shortstop's.

"But there are so many that are just alike, even yours," Prissy said to Junior.

"That's good," Junior said, moving down the row to the next bike like Shortstop's.

Why does Junior think it is good that so many bikes look alike? What is he doing?

CLAUDE VICIOUSLY

"The ringmaster insisted Claude Viciously use that new lion in his act because he was so big and aggressive—a crowd pleaser," Mrs. Viciously told Dr. J. L. Quicksolve as they sat in her trailer discussing her husband's death. "The lion wasn't trained. Claude was afraid of him. Claude hadn't been afraid in years, but this scared him. He sat right there, barely two hours ago at breakfast, and decided he wouldn't go in with the new lion unless he had his gun loaded. He was always proud that he could work with the big cats without even the blank pistol some trainers use. He was scared. Animals sense that, you know."

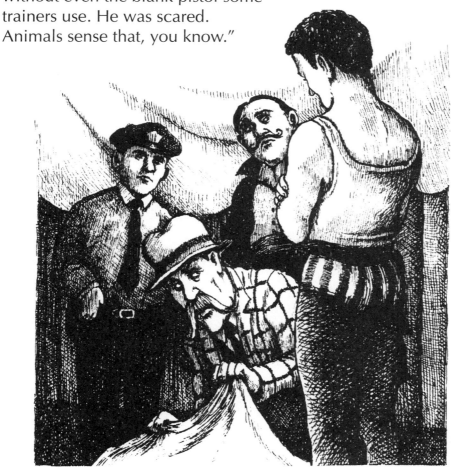

Claude's body lay in the center of the ring covered by a blanket. The lion had been put away, and Lieutenant Rootumout and two other men stood beside the body. One man, obviously the ringmaster, wore a fancy suit with long tails. The other, a performer, wore black tights and a bright red sash.

"I should not have insisted he use that new lion," the ringmaster said, clearly shaken by the death.

Lieutenant Rootumout held up a clear plastic bag as Dr. Quicksolve approached. It contained a large revolver. "It's empty," he said to Dr. Quicksolve.

"I can't believe he forgot the bullets," Stretch Prettitight said. "He was afraid of that lion."

Dr. Quicksolve bent down and lifted the edge of the blanket to look at the body. "Looks like murder," he said.

"Lions can't be charged with murder," Stretch scoffed.

"*You* can," Dr. Quicklove replied.

Why does Dr. Quicksolve suspect Stretch?

STORY BUILDERS

GENERAL INSTRUCTIONS

For these games, add a letter to the underlined letter or letters to complete the blank word that follows. Then, using the same letters, add still another letter to complete the next word, and so on. Letters may or may not appear in the same sequence each time, but each word will always contain the letters from the previous word in addition to the new letter you add.

Solutions—Page 247

1
THE REST IS UP TO YOU

"I T really is a shame to S i t around and feel that life is over because you had to retire," Mona admonished Jack. "In fact, it's the p i t s ! Why not find a hobby, read a book, or plan some _ _ _ _ _ _ ? Or maybe you should see our _ _ _ _ _ _ _ . I'm sure Father O'Malley can offer you some _ _ _ _ _ _ _ _ from your sorrow over getting too much rest."

2
A LEGEND IN HIS OWN MIND

"I simply D O not understand why you think you're better than everyone else," Ben mused, slowly shaking his head in wonder as he studied Eugene. "Let's face it, you eat, sleep, drink, and walk on the same _ _ _ that a common cur _ _ _ _ , yet you've always _ _ _ _ _ as someone superior. In my opinion, you'd make a perfect _ _ _ _ _ _ , Eugene, and I _ _ _ _ _ _ _ this character flaw the first time we met. The crown you were wearing was a dead giveaway!"

3
WHAT YOU SEE IS WHAT YOU GET

A T what point does a mediocre painting suddenly become a great work of _ _ _ ? Usually it happens when self-appointed critics start to _ _ _ _ and rave about a work's redeeming value, focusing on features that are invisible to most of us. In this way, they _ _ _ _ _ us to doubt our own judgment, and _ _ _ _ _ _ their power to influence our tastes and buying habits.

Obviously it takes a _ _ _ _ _ _ _ amount of self-confidence and strength to say, "My _ _ _ _ _ _ _ _ is as valid as yours, Mr. Critic, and many of those _ _ _ _ _ _ _ _ _ _ you're calling art aren't on a par with preschool finger painting!"

4
CHARLES DARWIN, PHONE HOME!

"<u>P A</u> , you've known me a long time," grumbled Ma, "and by now it should be obvious that I'm not __ _c_ __ to pay __ __ _f_ __ attention to all your foolish notions. You __ __ __ _p_ __ constantly about science and evolution, neither of which you know very well, and I find it very upsetting when you __ __ __ __ _t_ __ with theories like the one you mentioned yesterday: that man is the least intelligent __ __ __ __ __ __ __ of all!"

5
WINNER TAKES ALL

"To <u>B E</u> honest, Sam, you've disappointed me," Joey said. "You lost the __ __ __ , but your __ __ __ __ is still outstanding. Now you expect me to stand here with __ __ __ __ __ breath while you __ __ __ __ __ __ the ethics of gambling. Well, you can just forget it, pal, I refuse to be __ __ __ __ __ __ __ for putting the squelch on a welch!"

6
CAREER ORIENTED

"<u>N O</u> individual, not even a very bright __ __ __ , can give you a fool-proof formula for success, Marsha," Mike said patiently, "but even a __ __ __ __ like yours truly can offer some pointers. That company party we attended last night, for instance, makes me __ __ __ __ __ to think you won't get the promotion you're after. It just doesn't look good when you fall asleep on the shoulder of the __ __ __ __ __ __ you're sitting beside at dinner, especially when it's your boss. And I'm sure someone in his position __ __ __ __ __ __ __ the merit of promoting an employee who __ __ __ __ __ __ __ __ , 'I prefer that you call me Marsha,' when he asks if he can call you a cab!"

7
WHO ARE WE TO JUDGE?

"Hi, <u>P A</u>," the young man greeted his father. "I just ran into your old
__ __ __ , Judge Mann, and he was so __ __ __ __ I hardly recognized
him! I guess he saw me do a double-take, because he smiled and said,
'I'm not sick, my boy, just tired. I've been hearing so many __ __ __
__ __ lately, I sometimes find myself __ __ __ __ __ __ when key
witnesses are testifying! I won't be surprised if a higher court
__ __ __ __ __ __ __ a lot of my recent rulings.' Then he smiled wearily
and added, 'Perhaps we judges should have settled for being
__ __ __ __ __ __ __ __ . Then we could just listen to the accused's
confession, and leave the judgement to someone much more quali-
fied!"

8
A HARD ONE TO FATHOM

<u>A</u> walk along this lonely beach is __ __ mystifying as the __ __ __ that
watches us in cryptic green silence. Here, where countless __ __ __ __
have witnessed the __ __ __ __ __ and laughter of earlier generations,
few __ __ __ __ __ __ remain of times that were. It is this great sense
of aloneness, I think, that __ __ __ __ __ __ __ the mystique pertaining
to oceans, and maintains a certain mysterious appeal __ __ __ __ __ __
__ __ as the sea, herself.

9
FOOD FOR THOUGHT

Some believe that knowledge, <u>P E R</u> se, has no value unless it is shared.
Only then, thay maintain, can humankind __ __ __ __ its benefits. Every
good seed of thought that is sown and cultivated in the beds of fertile
minds then becomes a __ __ __ __ __ of wisdom. Thinkers, in turn,
can __ __ __ __ __ __ its benefits with others, expand upon it, and
perhaps someday __ __ __ __ __ __ __ it in new, exciting ways. Such
is the story of growth.

10
IN DEEP WATER

"Like it <u>O</u> <u>R</u> not, Harold," Hazel said, "I've manned these oars long enough. It's time for you to __ __ __."

Noticing how far they were to shore, he cagily replied, "Okay, but mark my __ __ __ __ , tomorrow you'll regret not getting more exercise."

"More? I'm already so tired that I'd __ __ __ __ __ if I suddenly had to swim," Hazel snapped. "But your concern makes me __ __ __ __ __ __ , Harold, wouldn't you be healthier if you occasionally exercised more than just your prerogative?"

"There you go," Harold hissed. "You always manage to turn our outings into total __ __ __ __ __ __ __ , and now you're doing it again!"

Matters only __ __ __ __ __ __ __ __ from that point, and their canoe trip became just another paddle between the sexes.

TAKE FIVE

GENERAL INSTRUCTIONS

In the grids that follow, fill in each box with an answer beginning with the letter above each of the five columns, and fitting the caregory at the left of each row. Try to list one answer in every box, although some boxes may have more than one correct answer.

Solutions—Pages 248-252

#1

	S	C	O	R	E
AMERICAN INDIANS	Sioux Susquehand	cherokee		Rappahannk	
ICE CREAM FLAVORS	strawberry	cookies n' cream	orange	rasberry	
BIBLICAL FIGURES	Saul	c	o	Ruth	Elijah Ezekiel
VEGETABLES	squash	carrot		radish	eggplant
COLORS	silver	cerulean	orange	red	electric blue

#2

	R	G	P	S	B
CHEESES	-Ricotta			-sharp cheddar	-Blue -Bree
FEMALE SINGERS	reba				
BODIES OF WATER	river				
MEN'S FIRST NAMES	ralph		poker		
CARD GAMES					

	D	A	B	S	P
STATE CAPITALS	Dallass Des Mains Dover	Alabamy Atlanta Anapolis	Boise BadenTowg Boston	Sacramento springfield st. Paul	Pheonix
CARTOON CHARACTERS	Daffy Duck Duey	Aluin	Buggs Bunny	scrooge Snoopy	Pluto
TELEVISION SOAP OPERAS					
PROFESSIONS	Doctor dentist dietrrihian	Architecht artist	-boss	Scientist social worker	politician
CARY GRANT MOVIES					

#4

	C	H	A	M	P
MOVIE TITLES					
NUTS					
TREES					
7-LETTER NOUNS					
PRO FOOTBALL PLAYERS					

200

#5

	W	S	C	B	R
PROFESSIONAL GOLFERS					
SEAFOOD					
TELEVISION NEWSCASTERS					
BROADWAY MUSICALS					
WORLD CAPITALS					

#6

	T	S	M	R	C
TELEVISION SLEUTHS					
FAIRY TALES					
CHILD STARS					
DANCES					
MODES OF TRAVEL					

	G	R	E	A	T
MOVIE STARS					
FLOWERS					
CAR/TRUCK MODELS					
FOREIGN COUNTRIES					
RIVERS					

#8

	C	M	O	G	S
SPORTS-CASTERS					
MIXED DRINKS					
BIRDS					
MINERALS					
CANDY BRANDS					

#9

M	A	D	E	N
PAST OR PRESENT WORLD LEADERS				
INVENTORS				
MAMMALS				
ELVIS PRESLEY SONGS				
OPERAS				

#10

	G	E	C	A	S
HERBS					
U.S. ASTRONAUTS					
MAGAZINES					
FRUITS					
POETS					

SOLUTIONS

TRICKY TRIOS

1 "EGR"

A score of 15 is fine; 18, first-rate; 22, fantastic!

begrime, begrudge, biodegradable, degrade, degranulation, degree, degression, disintegrate, egregious, egress, egret, integrand, integrate, integrity, integrodifferential, legroom, megrim, negritude, peregrine, regress, regret, regroup, segregate, telegram, telegraph

2 "OXY"

Find 12, you're batting 1.000; 15, you're an all-star; 17, you're a hall of famer!

boxy, deoxycorticosterone, deoxygenate, deoxyribose, doxy, doxycycline, epoxy, foxy, hydroxyl, oxyacetylene, oxyacid, oxycephaly, oxygen, oxyhemoglobin, oxymoron, oxysulfide, oxytetracycline, oxytocic, oxytone, oxyuriasis, proxy

3 "ADI"

Finding 60 words is dandy; 70, fantastic; 80, phenomenal!

adiabetic, adieu, adios, adipose, adit, amantadine, anadiplosis, arcading, armadillo, badinage, barricading, beading, beheading, besteading, brigadier, brocading, butadiene, cadi, caladium, cannonading, cascading, circadian, contradict, contradistinguish, degrading, eradicate, escalading, evading, extradite, fading, freeloading, gladiator, gladiola, gliadin, goading, gradin, grading, granadilla, haggadist, heading, hexadic, invading, irradiate, irradicable,

207

jading, kneading, lading, leading, loading, masquerading, monadic, muscadine, nadir, nomadism, paladin, palladium, paradigm, parading, paradise, peccadillo, persuading, pleading, radial, radiant, radiator, radical, radio, radiology, radish, radium, radix, readily, reading, sadiron, sadist, shading, sporadic, spreading, stadium, steadily, threading, toadies, tornadic, trading, tradition, traditor, treading, triadic, wadi, wading

4 "ERT"

Finding 75 words is good; 90, excellent; 100, extraordinary!

advertise, alert, aperture, appertain, ascertain, assert, avert, berth, bertha, certes, certain, certificate, certify, certiorari, chert, concert, concertina, concertino, concertmaster, concerto, controvert, convert, convertible, convertiplane, covert, culvert, desert, desertion, dessert, disconcert, divert, diverticulitis, diverticulosis, diverticulum, divertimento, divertissement, entertain, evert, exert, expert, extrovert, fertile, fertilizer, filbert, gilbert, hypertension, hyperthermia, hyperthyroid, hypertonic, hypertrophy, inadvertent, inert, insert, intertexture, intertribal, intertropical, intertwine, introvert, invertase, libertarian, libertine, liberty, nerts, obvert, offertory, overt, overtake, overtax, overthrow, overtime, overtone, overtop, overtrain, overtrick, overtrump, overture, overturn, pert, pertain, pertinacious, pertinent, perturb, pertussis, pervert, poverty, property, puberty, revert, sertularian, stertor, subvert, summertime, supertanker, supertax, supertonic, tertial, tertian, tertiary, travertine, undertaker, underthings, undertone, undertrained, vert, vertebra, vertebrate, vertex, vertical, verticillate, vertiginous, vertigo, vertu, watertight, wert, wintertime

5 "AZI"

A score of 10 is terrific; 12, great; 15, tops!

amazing, azide, azimuth, azine, blazing, brazier, brazilwood, crazier, dazing, fazing, feazing, gazing, glazier, grazing, hazier, lazier, magazine, razing, triazine

6 "OQU"

A score of 8 is par; 10, a birdie; 14, an eagle!

baroque, coquette, coquille, coquina, coquito, croquet, croquette, croquinole, eloquent, hydroquinone, loquacious, loquat, moquette, roque, roquelaure, toque

7 "ICO"

A score of 65 words is outstanding; 75, magnificent; 82 or better, pure genius!

alnico, anticoagulant, anticonvulsant, apricot, beccafico, bellicose, bicolor, biconcave, biconvex, bicorn, bicorporal, bicostate, calico, chalicosis, chalicothere, chico, chicory, corticoid, corticolous, corticospinal, dicotyledon, epicotyl, helicoid, helicon, helicopter, icon, iconoclast, iconography, iconoscope, iconostasis, lamellicorn, lexicology, lexicon, licorice, limicoline, longicorn, lumbricoid, machicolate, magnifico, manicotti, manticore, maricolous, medico, medicolegal, minicomputer, multicolored, nicotiana, nicotine, orthicon, particolored, physicochemical, picogram, picoline, picornavirus, picosecond, picot, picotee, politico, portico, ricochet, ricotta, rupicolous, saxicolous, semicolon, semicomatose, semiconductor, semiconscious, silicon, silicone, silicosis, stereopticon, technicolored, terricolous, torticollis, toxicogenic, toxicology, toxicosis, tragicomedy, tricolor, tricorn, tricostate, tricot, tricotine, unicolor, unicorn, unicostate, uricosuric, varicolored, varicose, varicotomy, ventricose, versicolor, vidicon, vorticose, wicopy

8 "LPH"

Locating 6 words is fantastic; 7, stupendous; 8, absolutely colossal!

alpha, alphabet, alphanumeric, alphosis, delphinium, dolphin, phenolphthalein, ralph, sulphur, sylph, telpher

9 "EME"

If you find 40, you're a sharpie; 48, you're brilliant; 55, you're a genius!

bereavement, cemetery, cement, cementite, confinement, deme, demeanor, dementia, demerit, demesne, demeton, emend, emerald, emerge, emergency, emeritus, emersion, emery, emetic, emeu, ephemeral, excrement, heme, hemelytron, hemeralopia, increment, irremeable, irremediable, memento, mincemeat, misdemeanor, nemertean, nemesis, pavement, phoneme, piecemeal, premedicate, premeditate, radioelement, rapprochement, redeemer, refinement, remedial, remedy, remember, retirement, scheme, seducement, seme, sememe, semester, siemens, spireme, statement, supplement, supreme, telemetry, temerity, theme, tremendous, treponeme, trireme, vehement

LETTER PERFECT

1

1. Transparent, 2. Tenement, 3. Turnabout, 4. Treat, 5. Tart, 6. Tenet, 7. Tacit, 8. Triplet, 9. Temperament, 10. Turncoat, 11. Tangent, 12. Transplant, 13. Turret, 14. Transient, 15. Tablet, 16. Truant, 17. Tourist, 18. Threat, 19. Taut, 20. Tent, 21.Trout

2

1. Earthenware, 2. Edifice, 3. Ensemble, 4. Evacuate, 5. Engrave, 6. Earthquake, 7. Eloquence, 8. Embezzle, 9. Enumerate, 10. Evidence, 11. Esplanade,

12. Exorcise, 13. Equate, 14. Eave, 15. Elapse, 16. Escape, 17. Excuse, 18. Elegance, 19. Epicure, 20. Encourage, 21. Espadrille, 22. Effervescence, 23. Educate, 24. Editorialize, 25. Elaborate

3

1. Liverpool, 2. Landfill, 3. Laurel, 4. Lysol, 5. Libel, 6. Lateral, 7. Lentil, 8. Logroll, 9. Label, 10. Liberal, 11. Lull, 12. Literal, 13. Lil, 14. Loyal, 15. Lethal, 16. Loll, 17. Lackadaisical, 18. Lapel, 19. Lyrical, 20. Local, 21. Logical

4

1. Nightgown, 2. Noggin, 3. Nonagon, 4. Nylon, 5. Nobleman, 6. Newton, 7. Neon, 8. Nitrogen, 9. Napkin, 10. Newman, 11. Notion, 12. Nubbin, 13. Noon, 14. Nation, 15. Nineteen, 16. Nixon, 17. Napoleon, 18. Nolan, 19. Newborn, 20. Nun, 21. Nelson, 22. Neutron, 23. Nickelodeon, 24. Nucleon

5

1. Haunch, 2. Horseradish, 3. High, 4. Hopscotch, 5. Hooch, 6. Hash, 7. Hogwash, 8. Howdah, 9. Hyacinth, 10. Hallelujah, 11. Hearth, 12. Hairsbreadth, 13. Halvah, 14. Hannah, 15. Hush, 16. Harrah, 17. Homograph, 18. Henceforth, 19. Hunch, 20. Hurrah, 21. Hugh, 22. Homestretch, 23. Health, 24. Hitch, 25. Hashish, 26. Hutch

6

1. Raconteur, 2. Receiver, 3. Rumor, 4. Rooster, 5. Rigor, 6. Rustler, 7. River, 8. Radiator, 9. Reindeer, 10. Rear. 11. Roar, 12. Ranger, 13. Redeemer, 14. Revolver, 15. Renoir, 16. Ruler, 17. Rancor, 18. Rathskeller, 19. Rudder, 20. Rambler, 21. Rather, 22. Rapier, 23. Recur, 24. Recover, 25. Render, 26. Radar, 27. Regular

7

1. Deceased, 2. Dachshund, 3. David, 4. Dilapidated, 5. Diamond, 6. Doodad, 7. Dryad, 8. Distend, 9. Devoid, 10. Dread, 11. Disregard, 12. Dividend, 13. Dagwood, 14. Dashboard, 15. Disneyland, 16. Dud, 17. Dead, 18. Deformed, 19. Dollywood, 20. Dad, 21. Descend, 22. Deed, 23. Discord, 24. Dastard, 25. Druid, 26. Demigod

8

1. Sacrilegious, 2. Spontaneous, 3. Spyglass, 4. Sophocles, 5. Stylus, 6. Suppress, 7. Superfluous, 8. Sans, 9. Sedulous, 10. Stress, 11. Symbiosis, 12. Stradivarius, 13. Sweepstakes, 14. Studious, 15. Sinus, 16. Scandalous, 17. Synopsis, 18. Slanderous, 19. Swiss, 20. Spineless, 21. Surreptitious

BATTLESHIPS

1

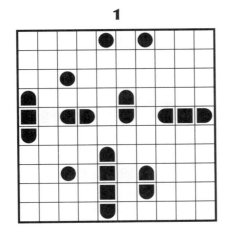

2

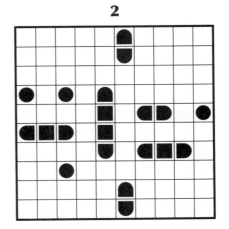

3

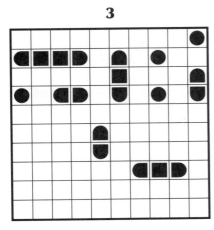

4

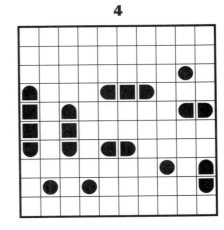

5

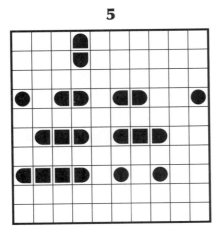

6

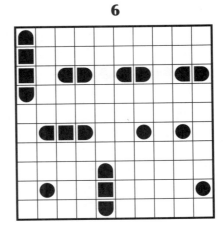

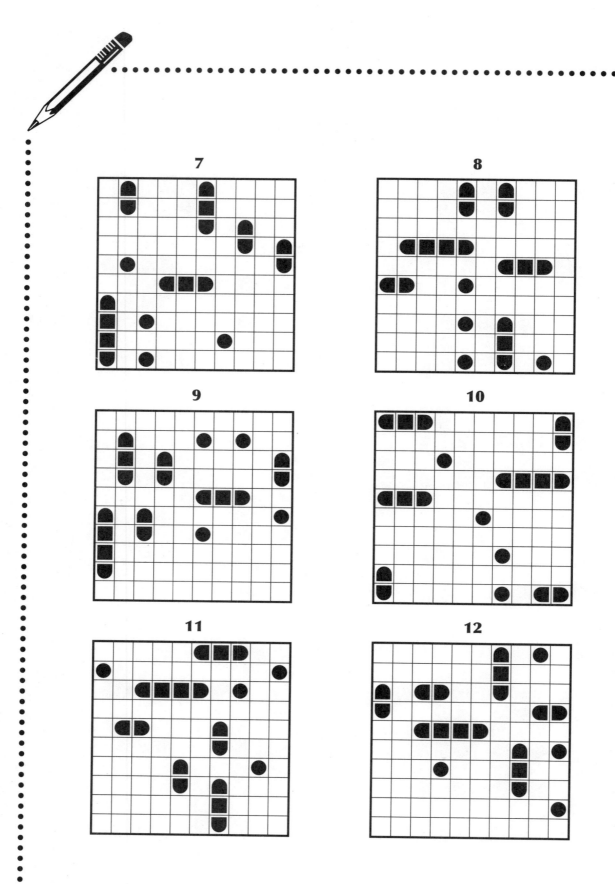

13

14

15

16

17

18

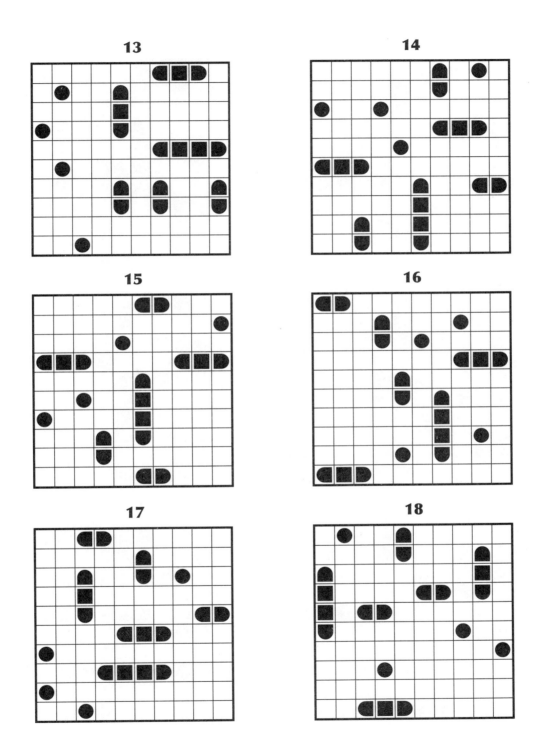

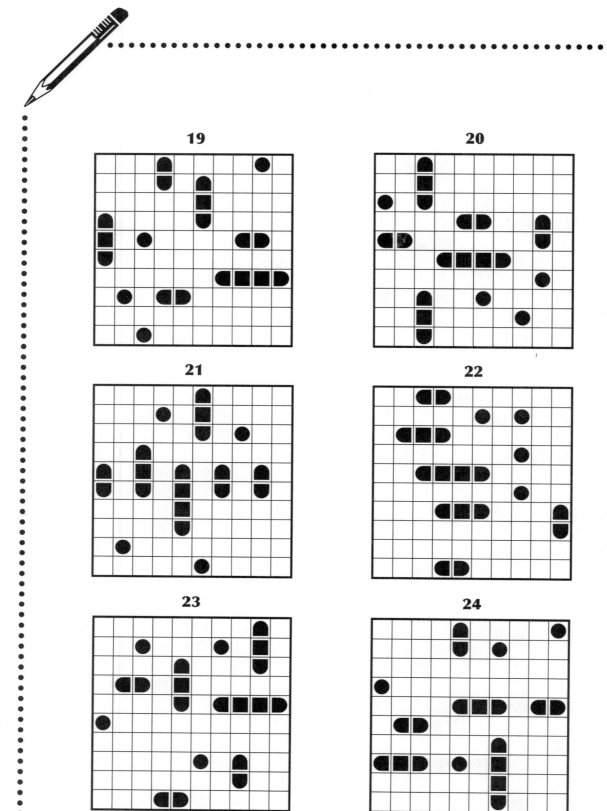

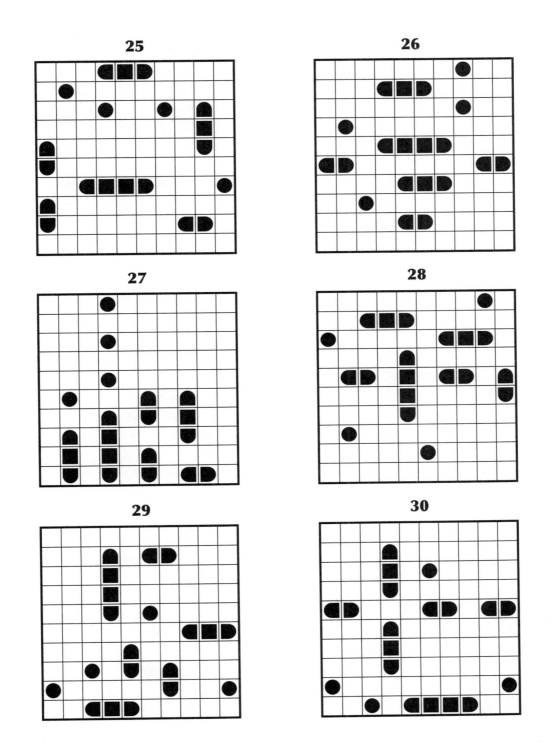

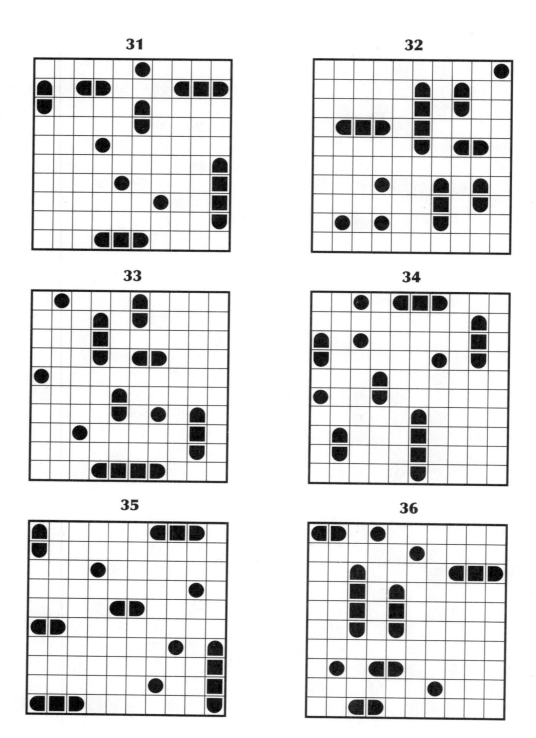

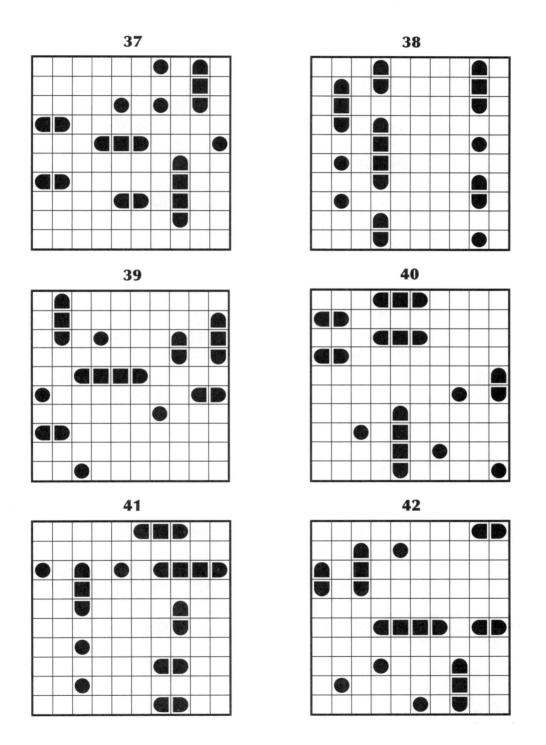

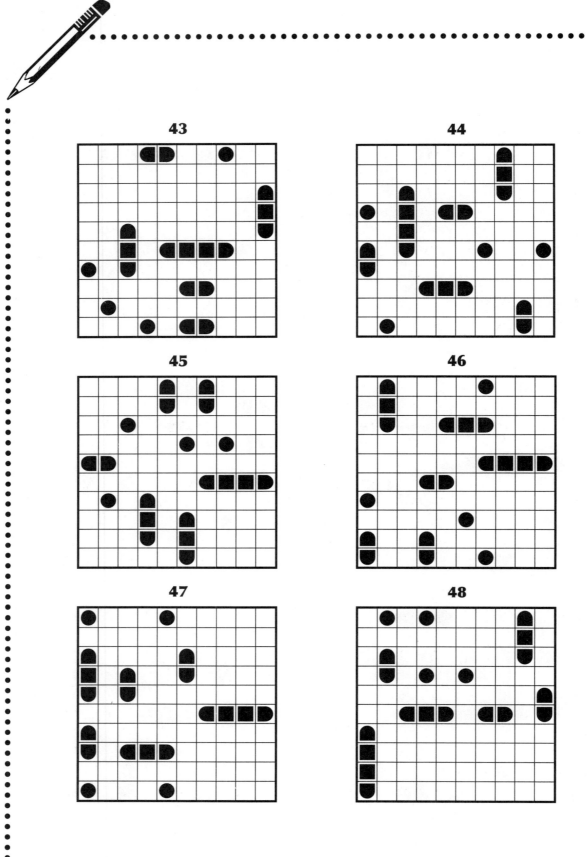

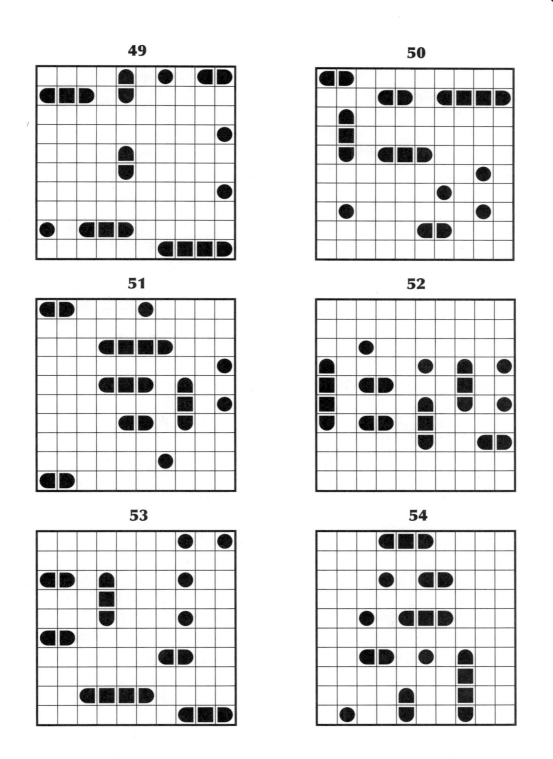

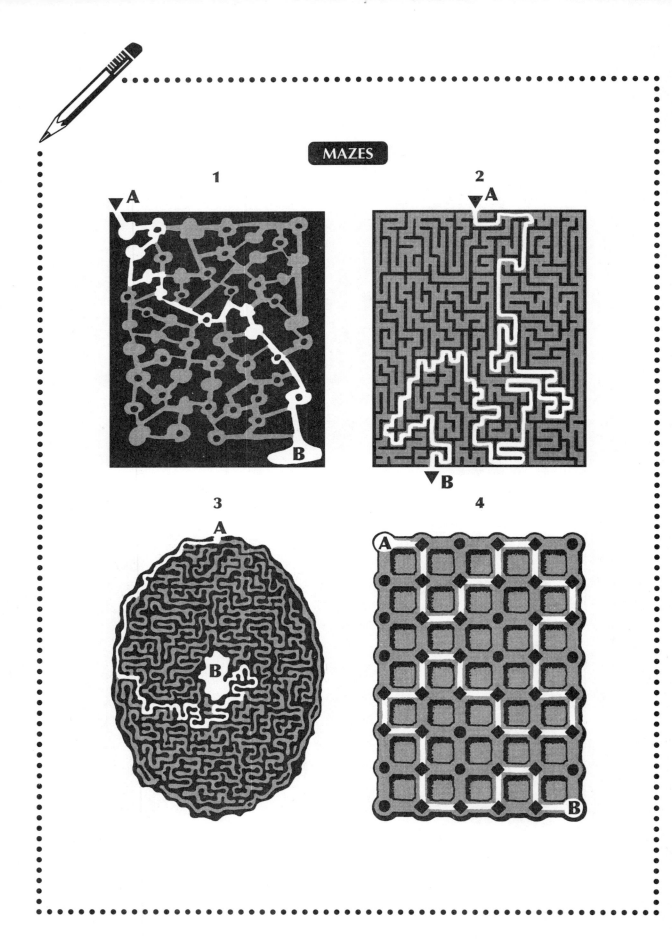

MAZES

1

2

3

4

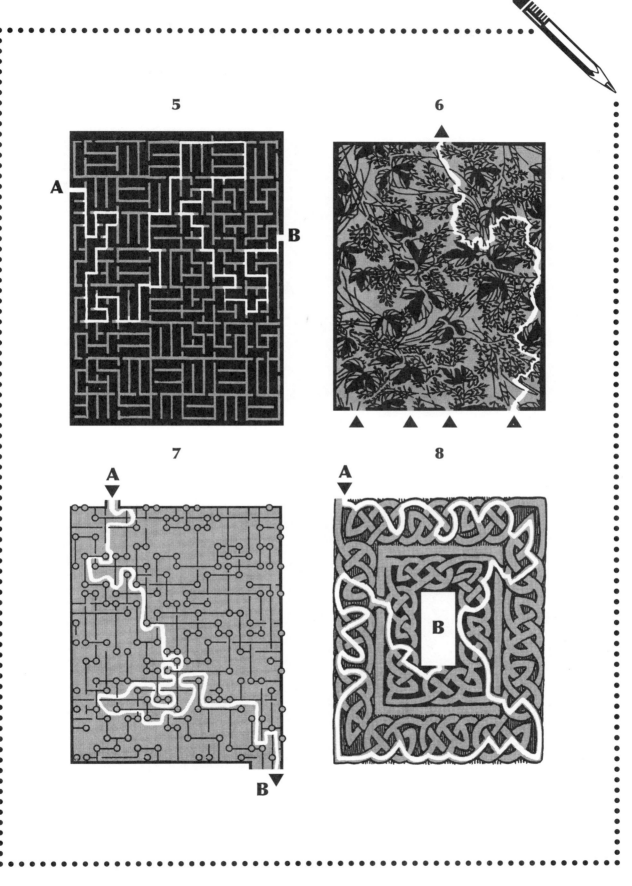

5

6

7

8

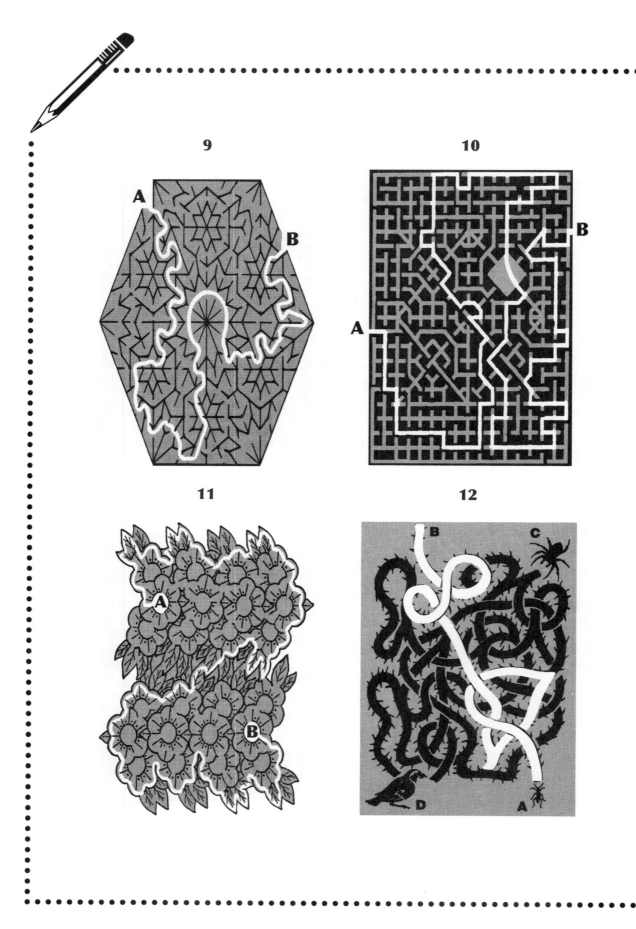

9

10

11

12

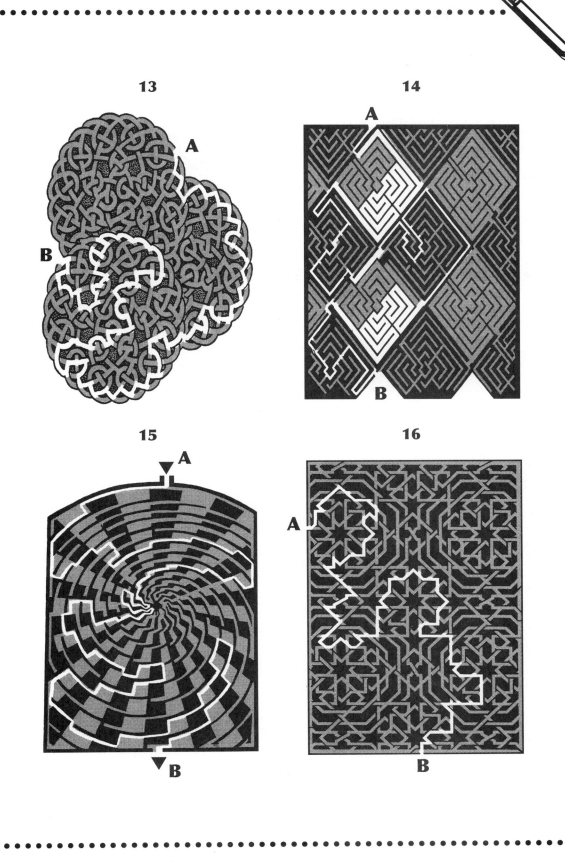

17

18

19

20

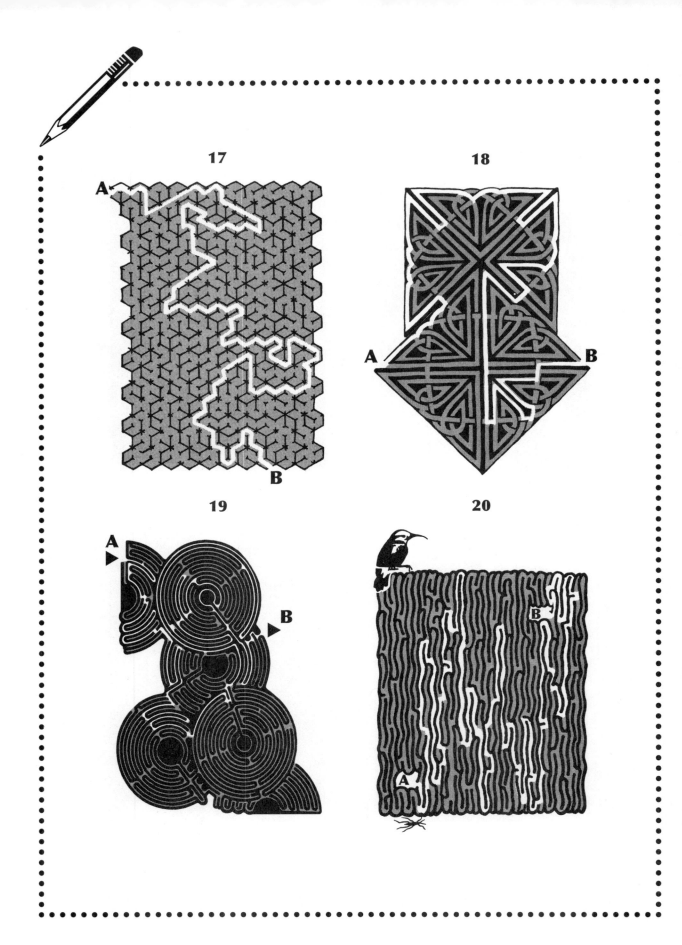

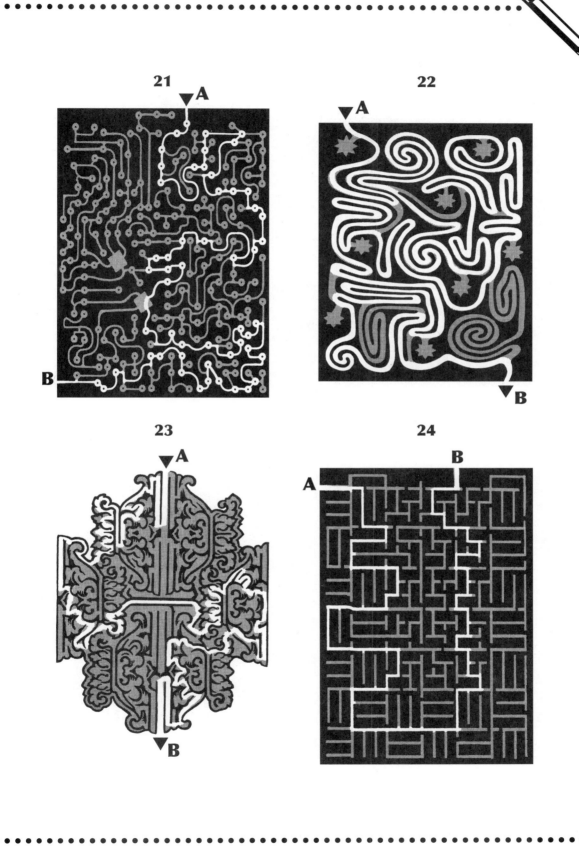

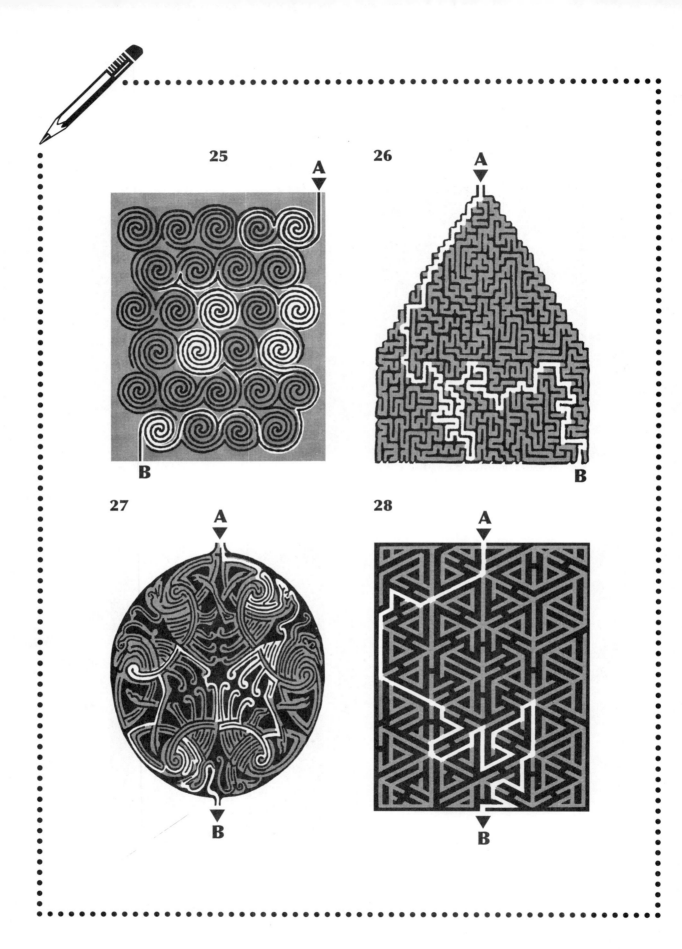

25

26

27

28

29

30

WHODUNITS

MURDER BETWEEN FRIENDS

Dr. Quicksolve suspected Tweeter. Her hearing seemed fine and her music was not loud enough to drown out the sound of gunshots. The hall was quiet and the music did not interfere with their conversation. She may have been angry with Terry for complaining about her music.

Many hearing-impaired people would be able to hear gunshots. Miss Blossom's Labrador was apparently a "hearing ear dog" who brought her to the door when Dr. Quicksolve knocked quietly. There is no reason to suspect Miss Blossom.

INHERITANCE

Dr. Quicksolve wanted to talk to the cousin from North Dakota because he had already eliminated the niece. The deceased, an only child and a bachelor, could not have a niece.

STRIKEOUT

Junior thinks Homer should not be trusted because he sells counterfeit baseball cards. Mickey Mantle played for the Yankees in 1951, so there cannot be a 1953 rookie card.

CODDLED COED

Sergeant Shurshot believes Holly took the money. She thinks Holly made up a quick alibi because no one with a cat in the house would leave unwrapped fish on the counter.

TELEPHONE RING

He expected to see a phone or credit card number on the pad that would match the number belonging to the man in the jacket. Dr. Quicksolve knew that thieves stand around open phones to listen while people say their card numbers into the phone. Then these criminals use the numbers to make calls or charge things. This time, the crook did not get away.

BEN BOINKT

Dr. Quicksolve doubts their story and wonders if Mr. Boinkt was hit at all. How could the robbers find the safe, open it, and be gone so quickly if Mr. and Mrs. Boinkt were both unconscious? He thinks Ben Boinkt and Glenda Cheatenhart killed Mrs. Boinkt.

SOCKS

Bobby said they were playing a team from Jackson. That means his was the home team, which would bat second and wouldn't bat the last inning if they were ahead after the visitors' last bat.

THE REAL MCCOY

Junior knew Blowhard's story about "the real McCoy" was not true. It is generally accepted that the expression is connected to an invention that automatically lubricates moving parts on many kinds of machines. The inventor was an African-American named Elijah McCoy.

BEN AGAIN

The fancy shooting and the long fistfight between the two men is hard to believe. The real problem with the story, though, is the wristwatch. There were wristwatches in the late 1800s, but they were designed only for women! Men used pocket watches at that time.

JOKERS WILD

Miss Forkton said she had just arrived home, yet her car was frosted over.

THREAT

The driver said they were looking at a map, yet he had not turned on the interior light to read it.

PLUNGER AND SNAKE

Plunger said someone hid behind the door. Dr. Quicksolve had just pulled the door open to come in. If the door pulled out to open, no one could have been hiding behind it on the inside.

SHORTSTOP'S BIKE

Because there are so many bikes that look alike, the thief would probably think it was safe to ride it to school, believing Shortstop could not identify his bike.

Junior and Shortstop had wisely etched their names inconspicuously under the crossbars of their bikes where no one would notice, but Junior could feel the engraving with his fingers.

CLAUDE VICIOUSLY

Being a circus performer, Stretch would have known lion tamers use blanks, yet he said "bullets." He only could have known there had been bullets in the gun if he was the one who took them out.

WORD SEARCHES

GUESS THE THEME 1 WORD LIST

BAGEL	NOSE
BELT	NOTEBOOK PAPER
BIRDHOUSE	PIERCED EAR
BUTTON	POCKET
CHEERIOS	SEWING NEEDLE
DONUT	SOCK
FLUTE	STRAINER
GOLF GREEN	STRAW
LIFE SAVERS	SWISS CHEESE
NETS	TIRE

GUESS THE THEME 2 WORD LIST

BEACH TOWEL	PAGE
BEDSHEET	PLACE MAT
COMIC STRIP	POSTCARD
COUPON	RECEIPT
DOMINO	RULER
DOOR	SHELF
ENVELOPE	STAMP
FLAG	TENNIS COURT
MENU	TWO-BY-FOUR
MOVIE SCREEN	WINDOWPANE

GUESS THE THEME 3 WORD LIST

AQUAFRESH	PARFAIT
BACON	PLAID
BARBER POLE	RACCOON
BAR CODE	REFEREE
BASS	SERGEANT
BILLIARD BALL	SKUNK
BUMBLEBEE	STRAW
CANDY CANE	TIES
CROSSWALK	TIGER
FLAG	ZEBRA

GETTING STARTED

Driver's advice: Engage mind before putting mouth in gear.

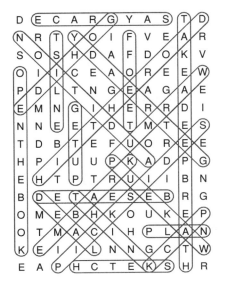

CHECK THIS OUT

If you play chess a lot, are you a chess-nut?

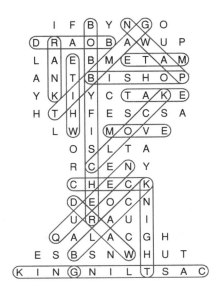

FATHER'S DAY

The best daddy would win a "pop"-ularity contest.

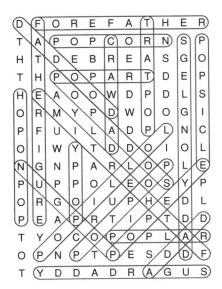

AT THE MALL

Tall Paul saw a scrawl on the wall at that small mall.

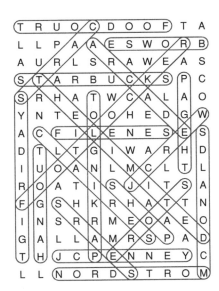

X MARKS THE SPOT

A boxer put the mix of Kix, Trix, and Rice Chex in the icebox.

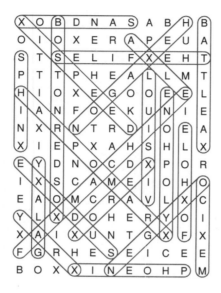

THE SIMPSONS

The space aliens who show up on occasion are Kang and Kodos.

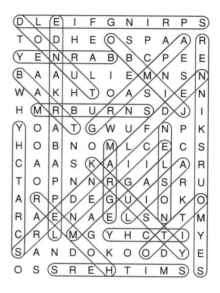

CIRCLING THE BASES

The youngest major leaguer was age fifteen.

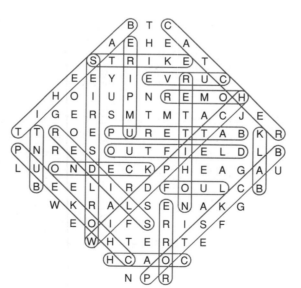

"IT'S ABOUT TIME!"

"Time is the most valuable thing a man can spend."—Theophrastus

AT THE MOVIES

At the movies, you pay to sit in the dark with a lot of strangers.

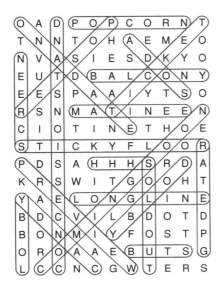

SURFING THE WEB

When a girl sends an electronic message, that's female e-mail.

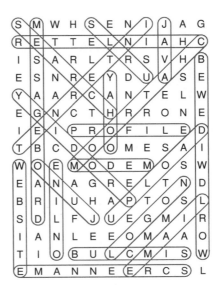

LIFE'S A PICNIC

A picnic means a fun time, a food-filled outing, or easy task.

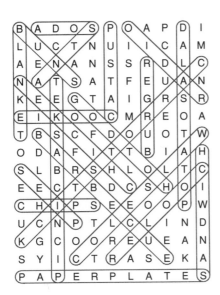

PIECE A PIZZA

No matter how you slice it, you have to admit this was easy as pie.

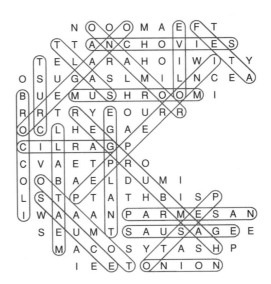

MONOPOLY GAME

Monopoly properties are named after streets in Atlantic City, NJ.

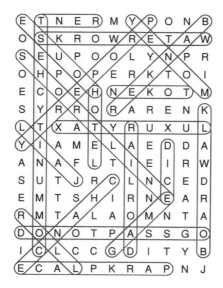

A BAND WE'D LIKE TO HEAR

"Music is the universal language of mankind."—Longfellow

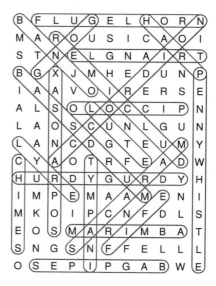

THINGS THAT SPIN

"We are spinning our own fates, good or evil."—William James

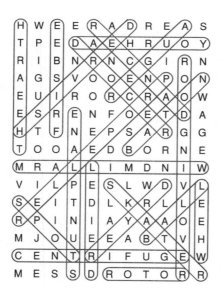

CAMP SIGHTS

Camp songs and scary stories are fun around the campfire.

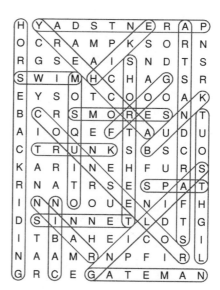

HINKY PINKY

Six hicks froze toes on the
Greek peak.

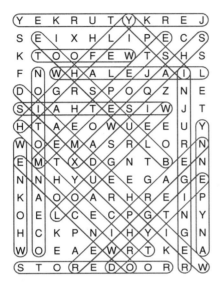

THE LEGEND OF ARTHUR

Arthur alone was able to pull the
sword out of the stone.

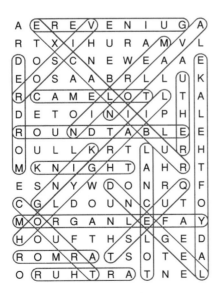

GUESS THE THEME 1

This Swiss cheese grid has things
with holes.

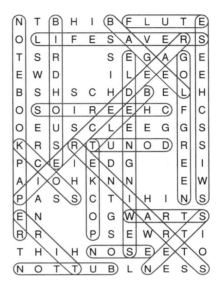

FEELING LUCKY?

Finding a heads-up penny is thought
to bring good luck.

IT'S ELEMENTARY

What do you get if you swallow uranium? You get atomic ache.

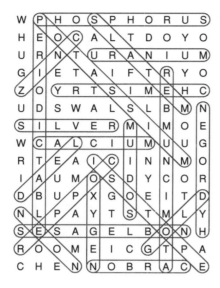

GUESS THE THEME 2

The grid and all the theme entries are usually rectangular.

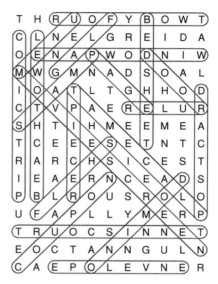

DOG AND CAT SCAN

When it's really pouring, we say it's raining cats and dogs.

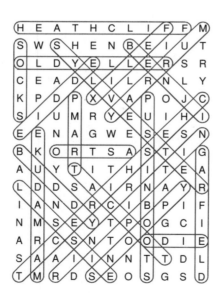

STAR WARS

The film "Spaceballs" was a spoof of "Star Wars."

"OH-OH"
Some other double O words are cuckoo, tattoo, Scrooge, and doodad.

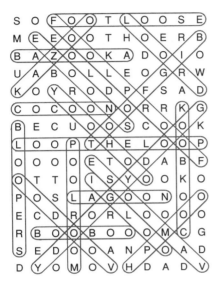

BEACHY-KEEN
Sandcastles require three things: sand, water, and imagination.

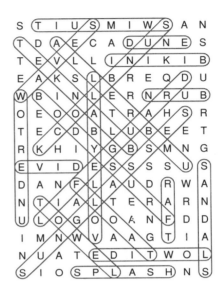

GUESS THE THEME 3
The grid is filled with items that always or often have stripes.

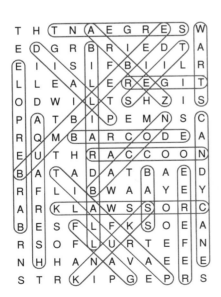

CASUAL DRESS
"Beware. . . all enterprises that require new clothes."—Thoreau

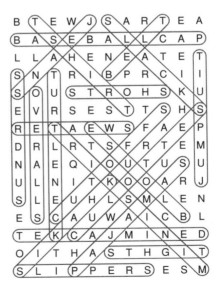

THE LOST WORLD

Not all dinosaurs were huge. Some were the size of a chicken.

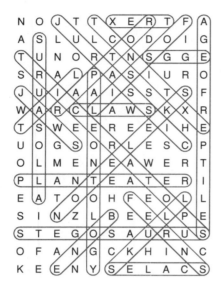

WRITE ON!

During a rite, it is right to write to Orville and Wilbur Wright.

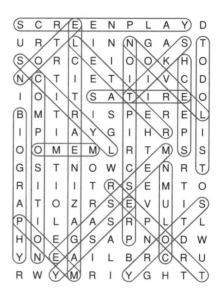

SCHOOL SUPPLIES

Supply costs can add up fast—using a calculator.

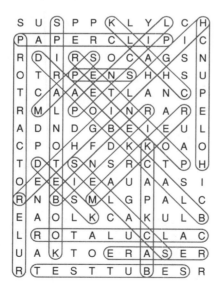

BY THE NUMBERS

The 3 Stooges called 911 to buy 1-way tickets on a Boeing 747.

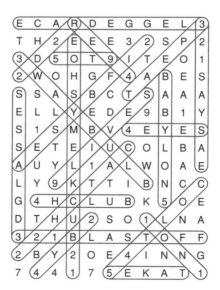

WORDWORKS

1 "GAMESTER"

(4 letters)

ages, arms, ease, east, game, gate, gear, gems, germ, geta, gram, mare, mart, mast, mate, meat, meet, mere, mete, rage, rags, rams, rate, ream, rest, sage, same, sate, seam, sear, seat, seem, seer, sera, sere, seta, stag, star, stem, tame, tare, tear, team, teem, term, tram, tree

(5 letters)

agree, ameer, aster, eager, eater, egest, egret, ester, gamer, grate, great, mater, merge, meter, reset, serge, smart, smear, stage, stare, steam, steer, tamer, tease, terse

(6 letters)

gamest, gamete, grease, master, meager, merest, stream, tamest, teaser

(7 letters)

steamer

2 "FAVORITE"

(4 letters)

aver, fair, fare, fate, fear, feat, feta, fiat, fire, five, fore, fort, frat, iota, over, rate, rave, reft, rife, rift, riot, rite, rive, rota, rote, rove, tare, taro, tear, tier, tire, tiro, tore, trio, vert, veto, vote

(5 letters)

afrit, after, avert, favor, forte, irate, orate, ovate, overt, ratio, rivet, trove, voter

3 "BETROTHAL"

(4 letters)

abet, able, alto, bale, bare, bate, bath, bear, beat, belt, beta, blat, blot, boar, boat, bola, bolt, bone, bore, both, brat, earl, hale, halo, halt, hart, heal, hear, heat, herb, hero, hoar, hoer, hole, hora, late, lath, lobe, lore, oath, oral, rale, rate, real, robe, role, rota, rote, tale, teal, that, tole, tort, tote, tret, trot

(5 letters)

abhor, abort, alert, alter, bathe, berth, betta, blear, bloat, broth, earth, heart, helot, hotel, labor, later, lathe, loath, obeah, orate, other, otter, table, tabor, taler, tarot, throb, throe, torte, total, treat, troth

(6 letters)

bather, batter, battle, bettor, boater, bolter, bother, bottle, breath, halter, hatter, herbal, hotter, lather, loathe, oblate, rattle, rotate, tablet, threat

(7 letters)

battler, betroth, blather, blotter, bottler, brothel

4 "DEVELOPMENT"

(4 letters)

deem, deep, dele, dent, dole, dolt, dome, done, dope, dote, even, lent, lode, lone, lope, love, meet, meld, melt, mend, mete, mode, mold, mole, molt, mope, mote, move, need, node, nope, note, omen, open, oven, peel, peen, pelt, pend, pent, plod, plot, poem, poet, pole, pond, pone, teem, teen, tend, toed, told, tole, tome, tone, tope, veep, vend, vent, veto, volt, vote

(5 letters)

delve, demon, depot, elope, emote, epode, event, lemon, levee, melon, model, motel, novel, olden, opted, peeve, tempo, tepee, veldt

(6 letters)

deepen, delete, demote, devote, needle, omelet, temple

(7 letters)

deplete, develop, devotee, element

(8 letters)

envelope

(9 letters)

elopement

5 "EXEMPLARY"

(4 letters)

aery, apex, army, axle, earl, eery, exam, lame, lamp, leap, leer, lyre, male, mare, meal, mere, pale, pare, peal, pear, peel, peer, perm, play, plea, pram, pray, prey, rale, ramp, rape, real, ream, reap, reel, rely, yare, year, yelp

(5 letters)

ample, amply, early, emery, expel, layer, leery, leper, maple, mealy, merle, payee, payer, pearl, pryer, realm, relax, relay, repel, reply, xylem

(6 letters)

leaper, merely, parley, pearly, player, replay

(7 letters)

example, lamprey

6 "POPULARITY"

(4 letters)

airy, alit, aril, arty, auto, lair, liar, lira, lory, lout, oily, opal, oral, pail, pair, palp, part, pita, pity, plat, play, plop, plot, ploy, port, pour, pray, proa, prop, pulp, pupa, puri, purl, rail, rapt, rial, riot, roil, ropy, rota, roup, rout, tail, tali, taro, tarp, toil, tolu, tori, tour, trap, tray, trio, trip, yaup, your, yurt

(5 letters)

aport, apply, aptly, atrip, laity, lapin, loppy, parol, party, patio, pilot, plait, platy, poilu, polar, polyp, pulpy, pupil, ratio, royal, trail, trial, troup, tulip, ultra

(6 letters)

artily, layout, outlay, papyri, parity, partly, payout, polity, poplar, portal, portly, purity, ripply, uppity

(7 letters)

popular, poultry, topiary

(8 letters)

polarity

7 "HISTORICAL"

(4 letters)

ails, alit, alto, arch, cart, cash, cast, char, chat, chit, clot, coal, coat, coil, cost, hail, hair, halo, hart, hoar, hora, host, iris, itch, laic, lair, lash, last, lath, liar, lira, list, loch, lost, oast, oral, orca, otic, rail, rash, rial, rich, roil, rota, sail, salt, sari, scar, scat, shot, silt, slat, slit, slot, soar, soil, sora, sort, star, stir, taco, tail, taro, this, tiro, toil, tola, tori, trio

(5 letters)

actor, ascot, chart, chili, choir, clash, cloth, coast, coral, crash, hoist, latch, loath, loris, ratio, roach, roast, salic, shirt, shoat, short, sloth, stoic, torch, trail, trash, trial, triol

(6 letters)

aortic, castor, choral, racist, sailor, silica, social, starch, thoria, thoric

(7 letters)

chariot, ostrich, trochal

(8 letters)

historic, holistic

8 "CONCENTRATION"

(4 letters)

acne, ante, cane, cant, care, cart, cent, coat, coin, coin, cone, coot, core, corn, cote, earn, icon, into, iota, iron, near, neat, neon, nine, nice, none, noon, note, oleo, olio, once, onto, oral, race, rain, rant, rate, rein, rent, rice, riot, rite, roan, rote, tact, tare, tarn, taro, tart, tear, tent, tier, tine, tint, tire, tone, torn, tort, tret, trot

(5 letters)

actor, antic, atone, attic, cairn, canoe, canon, canto, cater, caret, crane, crate, crone, croon, enact, inate, inert, inner, irate, nonce, octet, onion, orate, otter, ratio, riant, tacit, taint, tarot, tatoo, tenon, titan, toner, tonic, trace, tract, train, trait, trice, trine

(6 letters)

accent, action, arctic, attire, cancer, cannon, cannot, canter, cantor, carton, cornea, cornet, corona, cotton, crater, intact, nation, nectar, notion, octane, ration, retina, rotate, trance

(7 letters)

cartoon, conceit, concern, concert, connect, connote, contact, contain, content, contort, coronet, entrant, nictate, oration, raccoon

(8 letters)

contract, creation, interact, notation, reaction, rotation, traction

(9 letters)

container

(10 letters)

concertina, connection

(11 letters)

contraction

9 "XYLOPHONE"

(4 letters)

help, hole, holp, holy, hone, hood, hope, hypo, lone, loon, loop, lope, lynx, nope, only, onyx, open, oxen, peon, ploy, pole, polo, pone, pony, pooh, pool

(5 letters)

epoxy, honey, hooey, loony, peony, phlox, phone, phony, pylon

(6 letters)

holpen, openly, phenol, phenyl, phooey

10 "NASTURTIUM"

(4 letters)

amir, anti, aunt, main, mart, mash, mast, mina, mint, mist, mitt, must, mutt, nuts, rain, rani, rant, ruin, runt, rust, sari, sima, smut, snit, star, stir, stun, suit, sura, tain, tarn, taut, tint, tram, trim, tsar, tuna, turn, unau, unit, urus

(5 letters)

astir, manus, matin, minus, ramus, riant, saint, satin, sitar, smart, stain, start, stint, stria, strum, strut, stunt, suint, sutra, taint, taunt, train, trait, trust, unarm

(6 letters)

antrum, artist, autism, instar, mantis, martin, mutant, nutria, strain, strait, struma, tanist, truant

(7 letters)

intrust, stratum, transit, uranium

(8 letters)

transmit

11 "WHISPERING"

(4 letters)

egis, gens, grew, grin, grip, heir, hers, hewn, hire, news, pens, pews, phew, pier, pine, ping, pins, prig, ring, ripe, rise, sewn, shin, ship, sigh, sign, sine, sing, sire, spew, spin, swig, weir, when, whip, whir, wigs, wine, wing, wipe, wire, wise, wish, wisp

(5 letters)

gripe, hinge, pries, prise, reign, resin, rinse, ripen, risen, shine, shire, shrew, sinew, singe, spine, spire, sprig, swine, swing, weigh, whine, wring

(6 letters)

hewing, hiring, perish, resign, sewing, shiner, shrine, signer, singer, siring, spring, whiner, wiping, wiring

(7 letters)

inspire, swinger, wishing

(9 letters)

perishing

12 "POLITICIAN"

(4 letters)

alit, alto, anil, anti, cant, capo, clan, clap, clip, clop, clot, coal, coat, coil, coin, cola, colt, copt, icon, laic, lain, lint, lion, loan, loin, nail, opal, otic, pact, pail, pant, pica, pint, pion, pita, plan, plat, plot, taco, tail, talc, toil, topi

(5 letters)

actin, aloin, antic, canto, capon, coati, iliac, inapt, ionic, licit, nopal, ontic, optic, paint, panic, patio, piano, picot, pilot, piton, plain, plait, plant, plica, point, talon, tonal, tonic, topic

(6 letters)

action, cation, catnip, italic, oilcan, pliant, pontil

(7 letters)

capitol, caption, initial, pinitol, politic, topical

GREAT BEGINNINGS

1

1. Incentive, 2. Incognito, 3. Infallible, 4. Inn, 5. Invoice, 6. Intrepid, 7. Interloper, 8. Insomnia, 9. Inherit, 10. Inmate, 11. Infirmity, 12. Inch, 13. Injure, 14. Inert, 15. Interrogate, 16. Infant, 17. Incubate, 18. Inferno, 19. Indigo, 20. Indiana, 21. Infantry, 22. Indict, 23. Ink

2

1. Expel, 2. Exit, 3. Exempt, 4. Excellent, 5. Exaggerate, 6. Extra, 7. Exam, 8. Experiment, 9. Expression, 10, Excuse, 11. Exodus, 12. Expensive, 13. Exile, 14. Exact, 15. Excalibur, 16. Extraterrestrial, 17. Expand, 18. Exhaustion, 19. Expressway, 20. Executioner, 21. Export, 22. Extrovert

3

1. Quagmire, 2. Quartet, 3. Quilt, 4. Quack, 5. Quake, 6. Quiet, 7. Quarrel, 8. Quicksand, 9. Queen, 10. Quandary, 11. Quaker, 12. Quarantine, 13. Quail, 14. Quarry, 15. Quisling, 16. Quaff, 17. Quirk, 18. Query, 19. Queue, 20. Quaint, 21. Quell, 22. Quinine, 23. Quince, 24. Quarterback, 25. Quip

4

1. Wacky, 2. Wafer, 3. Waldorf salad, 4. Waft, 5. Waitress, 6. Wagon, 7. Waif, 8. Walrus, 9. Wallaby, 10. Walnut, 11. Wanton, 12. Wallflower, 13. Wax, 14. Wattle, 15. Wardrobe, 16. Washboard, 17. Warble, 18. Warpath, 19. Washington, 20. Warlock, 21. Wanderlust, 22. Waltz

5

1. Shadow, 2. Sherbet, 3. Shakespeare, 4. Shallot, 5. Shyster, 6. Shard, 7. Shroud, 8. Shirk, 9. Shrapnel, 10. Sham, 11. Shrine, 12. Shilling, 13. Shrug, 14. Sheriff, 15. Shrub, 16. Sheaf, 17. Shoat, 18. Shortening, 19. Shriek, 20. Shrimp, 21. Shrew, 22. Shun

6

1. Poetry, 2. Porcelain, 3. Poltergeist, 4. Polygraph, 5. Poach, 6. Poi, 7. Pontiff, 8. Portfolio, 9. Pollen, 10. Porcupine, 11. Portrait, 12. Posture, 13. Poker, 14. Poppycock, 15. Pompadour, 16. Polka, 17. Posse, 18. Polaris, 19. Politburo, 20. Pony Express

7

1. Mandate, 2. Marmoset, 3. Madrigal, 4. Marble, 5. Martian, 6. Majordomo, 7. Martyr, 8. Macaroni, 9. Mardi Gras, 10. Maneuver, 11. Maze, 12. Malaria, 13. Marsh, 14. Macbeth, 15. Marathon, 16. Manicure, 17. Mambo, 18. Martini, 19. Magenta

8

1. Foal, 2. Folly, 3. Forte, 4. Fondue, 5. Forgery, 6. Football, 7. Foe, 8. Footnote, 9. Forever, 10. Font, 11. Foliage, 12. Forest, 13. Forceps, 14. Foible, 15. Fodder, 16. Fob, 17. Forage, 18. Foundling, 19. Fortnight, 20. Fossil, 21. Forget-me-not, 22. Forbid

9

1. Noodle, 2. Nostalgia, 3. November, 4. Notch, 5. Noah, 6. Nominee, 7. Noxious, 8. Nonchalant, 9. Noise, 10. Novena, 11. Noel, 12. Nobel (Alfred), 13. Noose, 14. Nozzle, 15. Nom de plume, 16. Notary, 17. Nougat, 18. Note, 19. Nomad, 20. Nocturnal, 21. Novice, 22. North pole, 23. Nodule

SAY IT AGAIN, SAM

1

compliment, acclaim, praise, laud, commend

2

effort, endeavor, attempt, strive, try

3

adversary, rival, antagonist, enemy, predator

4

instruct, train, teach, educate, tutor

5

secret, enigma, mystery, riddle, puzzle

6

eject, evict, exclude, expel, oust

7

garbage, waste, trash, rubbish, refuse

8

consider, cogitate, deliberate, ruminate, ponder

9

mistake, omission, fallacy, blunder, error

10

implore, entreat, beseech, appeal, plead

STORY BUILDERS

1 THE REST IS UP TO YOU

it, sit, pits, trips, priest, respite

2 A LEGEND IN HIS OWN MIND

do, sod, does, posed, despot, spotted

3 WHAT YOU SEE IS WHAT YOU GET

at, art, rant, train, retain, certain, reaction, creations

4 CHARLES DARWIN, PHONE HOME!

pa, apt, rapt, prate, tamper, primate

5 WINNER TAKES ALL

be, bet, debt, bated, debate, berated

6 CAREER ORIENTED

no, one, peon, prone, person, ponders, responds

7 WHO ARE WE TO JUDGE?

pa, pal, pale, pleas, asleep, repeals, prelates

8 A HARD ONE TO FATHOM

a, as, sea, eras, tears, traces, creates, as secret

9 FOOD FOR THOUGHT

per, reap, pearl, parley, reapply

10 IN DEEP WATER

or, row, word, drown, wonder, downers, worsened

TAKE FIVE

1

	S	C	O	R	E
AMERICAN INDIANS	Seneca Shoshone Sioux	Cherokee Comanche Crow	Ojibway Osage	Ree Rikari	Erie
ICE CREAM FLAVORS	Strawberry	Chocolate	Orange	Raspberry Rocky Road	Eggnog
BIBLICAL FIGURES	Salome Saul Solomon	Cain Christ	Obadiah Ozymandius	Rachel Raphael Ruth	Esther Ezekiel
VEGETABLES	Spinach Squash	Cabbage Cauliflower Corn	Okra Onion	Radish Rutabaga	Eggplant Endive
COLORS	Scarlet Sienna	Cerulean Coral Crimson	Ochre Olive	Red Russet	Ebony Ecru

2

	R	G	P	S	B
CHEESES	Romano Roquefort	Gorgonzola Gouda	Parmesan Provolone	Saanen Swiss	Boursin Brie
FEMALE SINGERS	Helen Reddy Linda Ronstadt Diana Ross	Crystal Gayle Lesley Gore	Patti Page Dolly Parton	Carly Simon Grace Slick Barbra Streisand	Joan Baez Anita Baker Pat Benatar
BODIES OF WATER	Red Lake Red Sea Gulf of Mexico	Guanabara Bay	Pacific Ocean Persian Gulf	Salton Sea Sea of Cortez Strait of Magellan	Baltic Sea Bering Sea Black Sea
MEN'S FIRST NAMES	Ralph Richard Robert Roger	George Gilbert Grant	Paul Perry Peter Philip	Sal Simon Steve Stuart	Bill Bruce Bryan
CARD GAMES	Red Dog Rummy Russian Bank	Garbage Gin Go Fish	Parliament Pinochle Poker	Sixty-Six Skat Solitare	Baccarat Blackjack Bridge

3	D	A	B	S	P
STATE CAPITALS	Denver Des Moines Dover	Albany Austin Atlanta	Baton Rouge Bismarck Boise	Sacramento Salem Salt Lake City	Phoenix Pierre Providence
CARTOON CHARACTERS	Daffy Duck Donald Duck Dudley Doright	Archie Atom Ant	Betty Boop Bugs Bunny Bullwinkle	Scooby Doo Spiderman Superman	Pepe Le Pew Popeye Porky Pig

TELEVISION SOAP OPERAS	Dallas
	Days of Our
	  Lives
	Dynasty
		All My
		  Children
		As The World
		  Turns
			(The) Bold
			  and The
			  Beautiful
				Santa Barbara
				Search For
				  Tomorrow
					Peyton
					  Place

PROFESSIONS	Dancer Dentist Doctor Draftsman	Actor Astronaut Auctioneer Author	Baker Barber Bartender Butler	Salesclerk Scribe Shepherd Surgeon	Policeman Potter Preacher

CARY GRANT MOVIES	Destination
	  Tokyo
	Dream Wife
		(The) Awful
		  Truth
		An Affair to
		  Remember
			(The) Bishop's
			  Wife
			Bringing Up
			  Baby
				Suspicion
				Sylvia
				  Scarlett
					Penny
					  Serenade
					Philadelphia
					  Story

4	C	H	A	M	P

MOVIE TITLES	Casablanca
	(The) Color
	  Purple
	Cool Hand
	
	  Luke
		Harold and
		  Maude
		High Noon
		(The) Hustler
			Adam's Rib
			All About Eve
			Annie Hall
				Marnie
				Married to
				  the Mob
				Marty
				Moonstruck
					Parenthood
					Pinocchio
					The
					  Producers

NUTS	Cashew Castana Chestnut	Hazel Head Hickory	Acorn Almond Applenut	Macadamia Maranon Mast	Peanut Pecan Pistachio
TREES	Carob Cedar Chinaberry	Hardtack Haw Hickory	Alder Ash Aspen	Maple Mimosa Mulberry	Pecan Pine Poplar
7-LETTER NOUNS	Clothes Coaster Command Culvert	Handful Heathen History Hygiene	Admiral Alimony Ammonia Avarice	Mammoth Mineral Mongrel Monster	Pattern Playpen Poultry Primary

PRO FOOTBALL PLAYERS	Earl
	  Campbell
	Dwight
	  Clark
		Drew Hill
		Tony Hill
		Paul
		  Hornung
			Tony Aikman
			Marcus Allen
			Lyle Alzado
				Dan Marino
				Joe Montana
				Jim McMahon
					Drew
					  Pearson
					Dan
					  Pastorini

5	W	S	C	B	R
PROFESSIONAL GOLFERS	Tom Watson Tom Weiskopf	Gene Sarazen Sam Snead Curtis Strange	Billy Casper Bruce Crampton	Seve Ballesteros Julius Boros	Mike Reid Chi Chi Rodriguez
SEAFOOD	Walleye Whitefish	Salmon Scrod Sole	Catfish Cod Crayfish	Bass Bluefish Butterfish	Red Snapper Roughy
TELEVISION NEWSCASTERS	Mike Wallace Barbara Walters	Morley Safer Diane Sawyer Bernard Shaw	Connie Chung Walter Cronkite	Ed Bradley David Brinkley Tom Brokaw	Dan Rather Harry Reasoner
BROADWAY MUSICALS	West Side Story Wildcat	Show Boat South Pacific	Cabaret Cats (A) Chorus Line	Band Wagon Brigadoon Bye Bye Birdie	Rhapsody Rumple
WORLD CAPITALS	Warsaw Washington, D.C.	San Salvador Santiago Sydney Singapore	Cairo Caracas Copenhagen	Brasilia Brussels Bucharest Budapest	Reykjavik Rome

6	T	S	M	R	C
TELEVISION SLEUTHS	Dan Tannna Vinnie Terranova Harry S. Truman	Maxwell Smart Remington Steele B.L. Stryker	Thomas Magnum Mannix McCloud	Rockford	Cannon Columbo Dale Cooper
FAIRY TALES	Three Little Pigs	Snow White and the Seven Dwarfs	Mother Goose	Rapunzel	Cinderella
CHILD STARS	Elizabeth Taylor Shirley Temple	Fred Savage Ricky Schroeder Brooke Shields	Jerry Mathers Hayley Mills Kurt Russell	Mickey Rooney	Kirk Cameron Jackie Coogan
DANCES	Tango Twist	Samba Square Dance Swim	Mambo Mashed Potato Monkey	Reel Rumba	Cancan Cha-Cha Charleston Conga
MODES OF TRAVEL	Taxi Train Tricycle Trolley Car	Skateboard Space Shuttle Subway	Moped Motorcycle	Raft Rickshaw Rocket ship Rowboat	Canoe Car Caravan Carriage

7 — G R E A T

	G	R	E	A	T
MOVIE STARS	Clark Gable Greta Garbo Cary Grant	Robert Redford Christopher Reeve	Emilio Estevez Dame Edith Evans Tom Ewell	Alan Alda Julie Andrews Dan Aykroyd	Rip Torn Spencer Tracy Kathleen Turner
FLOWERS	Gardenia Geranium Gladiolus	Rhodora Rose	Edelweiss Elite Essence	Amaryllis Aster Azalea	Truss Tulip Tutty
CAR/TRUCK MODELS	Grand Prix Gremlin Grenada	Ram Ranchero Regal	Eagle Edsel Excel	Accord Ambassador Aries	Taurus Torino Toronado
FOREIGN COUNTRIES	Germany Great Britain Greenland	Romania Russia Rwanda	Egypt El Salvador Ethiopia	Albania Algeria Argentina	Taiwan Tunisia Turkey
RIVERS	Ganges Gila Green	Rhine Rhone Rio Grande	Ebola Elbe Euphrates	Allegheny Arkansas Avon	Thames Tiber Truckee

8 — C M O G S

	C	M	O	G	S
SPORTS-CASTERS	Harry Carey Bob Costas	John Madden Jim McKay Al Michaels Brent Musberger	Pat O'Brien	Joe Garagiola Frank Gifford Greg Gumbel	Dick Stockton Pat Summerall
MIXED DRINKS	Cape Cod Cuba libra	Mai Tai Manhattan Martini Mimosa	Orange Fizz	Gimlet Gin & Tonic	Sloe Gin Fizz Screwdriver
BIRDS	Canary Cardinal Chickadee Crow	Meadowlark Mockingbird Mynah	Oriole Osprey Ostrich Owl	Goldfinch Goose Grebe Grouse	Sandpiper Sparrow Starling Swallow
MINERALS	Cinnabar Copper Corundum Cryolite	Malachite Mica Microline	Oroide Orthoclase	Gold Graphite Gypsum	Silica Sulfur
CANDY BRANDS	Cadbury's Caramello Charleston Chew Cherry Mash	Mars Bar Milk Duds Mr. Goodbar	O Henry	Good & Plenty Goo Goo Cluster	Snickers Sugar Babies

9	M	A	D	E	N
PAST OR PRESENT WORLD LEARDERS	Meir Mubarak Mulroney Mussolini	Adenauer Attlee	De Gaulle De Valera	Eben Eisenhower	Nehru Nixon Noriega
INVENTORS	Samuel Morse Guglielmo Marconi	Nicholas Appert Howard Aiken	John Deere Leonardo Da Vinci	George Eastman Thomas Edison	Alfred Nobel Thomas Newcomen
MAMMALS	Marmoset Mongoose Monkey	Aardvark Anteater Antelope	Deer Dik Dik Dog	Eland Elephant Elk	Narwhal Numbat
ELVIS PRESLEY SONGS	Make Me Know It	Are You Lonesome Tonight All Shook Up	Don't Be Cruel Devil in Disguise Don't	Easy Come, Easy Go End of the Road	Night Rider
OPERAS	Madam Butterfly (The) Marriage of Figaro	Aida Alcina Andrea Chenier	Don Carlos Don Giovanni	Elektra Eugene Onegin	Nabucco Norma (The) Nose

10	G	E	C	A	S
HERBS	Garlic Gentian	Elder Eryngium	Chervil Chicory Cumin	Alecost Angelica	Saffron Sage
U.S. ASTRONAUTS	John Glenn Virgil Grissom	Don Eisele Anthony England	Scott Carpenter Michael Collins	Buzz Aldrin Neil Armstrong	Walter Schirra Alan Shepard
MAGAZINES	GQ Glamour Gourmet	Ebony Elle Esquire	Cook's Country Living Car & Driver	Advertising Age Architectural Digest Auto Age	Southern Living Sports Illustrated
FRUITS	Grape Grapefruit Guava	Elderberry	Cherry Coconut Cranberry Currant	Apple Apricot	Strawberry
POETS	Kahlil Gibran Thomas Gray Robert Graves	T S Eliot Ralph Waldo Emerson	Samuel Coleridge e.e. cummings	Conrad Aiken W H Auden	Carl Sandburg Sir Walter Scott

INDEX

Page references to solutions are in italics.